The Month of Saint Michael

Saint Michael According to the Bible

and

According to Tradition

By Fr. Marin de Boylesve, S.J.

Saint Michael According to the Bible

and

According to Tradition

Readings for Each Day of the
Month of Saint Michael

By Fr. Marin de Boylesve, S.J.

Translated and Annotated by E.A. Bucchianeri

Batalha Publishers
Fatima, Portugal

This first English translation edition is based on the 1882 edition published by René Haton of Paris. The translation, added biography of the author, annotations and appendix by E.A. Bucchianeri, © 2021-2022 by Batalha Publishers, Portugal. Appendix features traditional Roman Catholic prayers and quotations in the public domain.

ISBN: 978-989-96844-92

Table of Contents

Saint Michael According to the Bible

Saint Michael According to Tradition

APPENDIX

Other Associations, Sacramentals and Prayers

About this Edition

As far as I am aware, this is the first time the French devotional booklet of St. Michael by Fr. Marin de Boylesve has been translated into English. The edition used for this translation was published in 1882 by René Haton of Paris. British spelling has been used in this translation. While faithful to the original devotional text this new English edition features several changes and additions: biography of the author, illustrations, plus the addition of informative notes and footnotes with explanations not included by Fr. de Boylesve. When required, these new notes will be indicated with my initials. An Appendix has been added featuring new material and other traditional devotions to St. Michael not included in the original book.

E.A. Bucchianeri

About the Author

Fr. Marin de Boylesve was born on November 28, 1813 at the Château de la Coltrie in the commune of Saint-Lambert de la Potherie near Angers. He came from a distinguished aristocratic family whose name can be traced back many centuries as seen in Abbé Jean-Baptiste Ladvocat's *Dictionnaire historique portatif* (1755). Fr. Marin descended directly from Eslienne Boyliaue (or Boilyeve), the great statesman and the principal adviser of St. Louis IX, King of France. Other illustrious ancestors included intrepid knights, one in particular also named Marin joined the cause of King Henry IV. After the Battle of Arques, the king called him 'his beloved knight', granted him a heredity knighthood in 1597, then was made Seigneur de la Maurouziere in 1598 thereby granting him the right to add three gold fleur-de-lis to the top of his arms and bear the signs of the Order of St. Michel in his escutcheon. He was also appointed lieutenant-general of Anjou and councillor of state as a reward for his dedication. Another Marin Boylesve appears in the family line, the third to hold the name, and was in service to King Louis XIV as manager of his hôtel. Loyal to the French King and to their Catholic faith, many members of the family were forced to emigrate during the French Revolution, but some members stayed behind in their beloved France. Fr. de Boylesve would recall a favourite family story, of how his grandmother was imprisoned in Angers by the Revolutionaries and managed a daring escape on the road during a prisoner transfer to the local castle. While she pretended to pick up a dropped package, a solider kicked her into the ditch. She took the opportunity to flee to a nearby house. However, when they threatened to imprison those harbouring escaped prisoners, she bravely marched straight in to the Revolutionary Office and gave herself up to ensure the safety of those who sheltered her. The revolutionaries did not dare risk upsetting the populace as her father was the former mayor of Angers before the Revolution and loved by the people. They decided to let her return to her father's house.

Fr. de Boylesve was the last direct descendant of his distinguished line, having followed the call to enter the Company of Jesus, or Jesuits, which also is a remarkable story of a predestined vocation. The Jesuits were persecuted due to fears they were growing in power and wealth. Pressured by the royal courts of Europe, Pope Clement XIV suppressed the Society, forcing members of the order to renounce their vows and go into exile. They were expelled from France in 1764. Fr. de Boylesve's mother, Clémentine de Livonnière, made a solemn promise on the day of her wedding that if God permitted the Jesuits to return to France and she was granted a son, she would offer him to the order and entrust him to it. As mentioned, Fr. Marin was born in 1813, a year before 1814 when Pope Pius VII restored the Society. Tragedy struck when Marin's father died, Marin was only ten months old at the time, but keeping her promise his mother dutifully sent him for his education at the age of ten to the Jesuit Fathers of Montmorillon. The moment he arrived at the school and saw a Jesuit for the first time who happened to be the Superior of the college Fr. Michel Le Blanc, he heard an inner voice say to him: "Little one, that is what you will be."

Fr. de Boylesve entered the school as a student and was destined never to leave the Jesuits. In 1831 he turned eighteen, a year after the July Revolution of 1830, which saw the rightful king to the French throne Charles X overthrown. His heir, Henry V the 'Miracle Child', was forced into exile at the age of ten, his throne usurped by the man who had been approached to be his regent, Louis-Philippe, Duke of Orléans. The events of the times burned the hearts of the faithful as the historical church of the royal family, Saint-Germain-l'Auxerrois, was profaned. Paris was sacked, and wayside devotional crosses and shrines over large areas of France were destroyed as Catholic legitimist symbols of Charles X, even those which had no royal significance or connection to the king.

Fr. Marin had just completed his schooling when he formally announced his decision to enter the Society, the historic events of the previous year and their aftermath no doubt influencing his decision. Writing to his grandmother he declared:

"The course of my studies completed I could not remain without doing anything. God will ask us for an exact account of all the moments He gives us. Full of this thought I ardently wished to serve my country and the Church especially. At a time when both are in such great peril, as a Frenchman and as a Christian, I felt the need to throw myself into the thick of the fray. To take place in the first rows under the banners of religion whose triumph alone can bring glory and happiness back to my homeland, to serve immediately under my first head Jesus Christ, to be one of His companions, seemed to me the most glorious at the same time as most useful for my neighbour. Immense advantages, treasures of happiness and glory, the hundredfold from this life of all that I would give to the Lord, all of these promised in the gospel by Jesus Christ, strongly attracted me to be generous. What more could I do than give myself? (...)"

His family strongly opposed, especially as he was the last direct heir to the Boylesve house, but his mother let him go despite the great sacrifice, no doubt she understood God was accepting her promise to give him to the Jesuits, and not just for his education but now was asking for his whole life, a bitter dreg for her down to the last drop of the cup.

He entered the Novitiate in 1831 at

Estavayer in the canton of Fribourg in Switzerland with two other students. As they arrived at their new school, they rang the doorbell at the moment the house clock struck three. The Father who received them remarked: "You are entering at the hour of the Sacred Heart." This introduction to a new school would once again give Fr. de Boylesve a sign regarding the future work he would one day accomplish, although on this occasion he did not know it at the time. He made his first vows at the Maison du Passage on October 10, 1833. He studied philosophy and then in 1835 became a supervisor at the Collège de Mélan, a position he held for one year. He remained in the same college until 1842 where he was in succession professor of grammar, humanities and rhetoric. He thoroughly enjoyed his work with the students, writing in 1837:

"I find this job a lot of fun, despite the hardships that come with it. I have forty students; I love them and I try to spare nothing to make them good Christians, educated Christians capable of one day rendering true service to religion and to the state. It is the sight of such a noble ending that sustains and animates me." In the same letter he continues, regarding his concern for his family, "(…) what the only important thing is, is everyone behaving well and does he remember the motto of the family, RELIGIO, PATRIA? For me who gave up everything, even my name which will be extinguished in my person, I remember it, and

God grant that I am consumed and that I use myself in the service of one and of the other."

Although renouncing his aristocratic life he never gave up its noble spirit represented by the family motto, an ardent loyalty to the Catholic faith of his forefathers and his country. In the title pages of his texts he included the family crest of three crosses and motto: RELIGIO, PATRIE – "Faith and Country". Those who knew him and his 'military' style ways said he was just like the loyal intrepid knights of old.

At the end of 1842 he returned to France. He took theology courses at Laval for four years. Instinctively he was drawn to the writings of St. Thomas Aquinas and steered clear of new systems that deviated from the philosophical teachings of the Seraphic Doctor. In 1846 theology training completed, Fr. Boylesve was sent by his superiors to Angers, then in his third year at Notre-Dame d'Ay. In 1848 he was appointed to Brugelette, where he occupied the chair of philosophy. One student who fondly recalled Fr. de Boylesve and his time at Brugelette said his arrival was providential. His classes were easy to follow his manner clear and crisp, but this is not all that gained the respect of the students. In 1848 they were restless as revolution was in the air, Louis-Philippe I, who had overthrown Catholic King Charles X was now in his own turn overthrown. Rising above and beyond what was required of his philosophy courses, Fr. Boylesve seized the opportunity like a knight-commander of old to direct the lazy students yet bursting with energy towards something constructive: Catholic action to fashion them into vigorous young men of service for Church and country. With his apostolic action he captivated the students with his literature classes, speaking on many subjects from philosophy, history, politics both ancient and modern. He particularly drew them with his catechism lessons on the Council of Trent, his clarity and enthusiasm captivating them.

As Fr. de Boylesve loved his students he was equally admired and loved by them, earning the nickname 'The Captain' as a mark of respect. The students composed a military style tune for his birthday, the refrain remaining popular and hummed everywhere: "Courageous Captain, lead us into battle." A student recalls: "I understood all that was apostolic about his action on us. We can sum it up by saying that he made it his mission to preach to us always and everywhere the contemplation of Saint Ignatius on the Reign of Jesus Christ as it is given in the Exercises." In 1851 Fr. Boylesve was sent to Vannes where he was made prefect of studies, his nickname 'The Captain' following him. In October 1853 he left the post and resumed teaching philosophy, a position that he would keep for a long time, either in Poitiers or in Vaugirard.

Known to be quiet and reserved when on his own, it was another matter when he was teaching or publicly speaking. He was incapable of remaining silent or softening his direct manner of expression when it was a question of truth, and did not hold back when it came to defend the Faith and the Church against unbelievers, becoming as noted like his knight-ancestor of old, charging forth to give chase and defeat any bold rascal on the field of battle albeit with his tongue and writings rather than with a literal sword. His attitude is quaintly displayed by the art critique he once gave of the statue of the fountain of St. Michael in Paris, complaining with slight annoyance that the mighty archangel was made to look too carefree and benevolent when dispatching Satan: "See then, it is that he seems to spare him!"

Fr. Marin was also a zealous worker and relished activity. He once wrote: "I challenge my superiors to give me too much work." In addition to his religious duties and teaching, he was a prolific writer, his output seeming to have no end. He wrote on a myriad of subjects and in different genres, from devotional booklets and pamphlets to history, literature, philosophy, Biblical dramas, summaries of the Church Fathers and Doctors, his own sermons, studies of the Scriptures, Our Lady, the Exercises of St. Ignatius just to name a few, there were always more plans for further works in progress, his room filled with notes and notebooks. He was always studying as well, also making it a practise to read through the entire Bible every year. One might call him a workaholic in today's terms, but it was noted he believed in a time and a place for everything and diligently managed his hours. He enjoyed recreation time, especially going for walks, and did not sacrifice rest. Despite his zest for work, he disapproved of a few young professors who sacrificed too much sleep and recreation time for their studies, endangering their health. Yet, while sparing of his time he was ever charitable and ready to help another all for the glory of God.

In September 1870 Fr. de Boylesve was sent to the College of Le Mans, Notre-Dame de Sainte-Croix, when the Franco-Prussian war was raging and France suffered the indignity of invasion. The humiliation felt by the country also struck the pious and patriotic Fr. de Boylesve to the core: "I searched through the memories of my life; I do not remember ever having felt greater pain than this, not even when I learned of my mother's death. This humiliation of France, the eldest daughter of the Church, thus succumbing before Prussia, the eldest daughter of Protestantism, in the face of the whole world, is something unheard of."

The Messenger, the magazine of the Apostleship of Prayer run by the Jesuits, began spreading the visions of St. Margaret Mary, declaring the only way France would be saved from her enemies was to embrace the devotion to the Sacred Heart. The message inspired Fr. de Boylesve. He became a chaplain to the Catholic Papal Zouaves forces sent to defend the French Motherland from the Protestant invaders, giving them rousing sermons: "Clotilde, inspiring faith in Clovis, saved the Franks and slaughtered the Germans at their feet ... Joan of Arc by her standard delivered France from the English! Your standard is the Sacred Heart." The Zouaves placed the Sacred Heart on their banner. Fr. de Boylesve also busily spread Sacred Heart badges of wool for the soldiers to pin on their uniforms, for they were in high demand. A gifted and inspiring preacher, his sermons encouraged them onward, even when they were driven back in defeat by the Prussians to where the soldiers remarked: "This man can lead us to the fire tomorrow; we would gladly be killed for him."

Fr. de Boylesve is fondly remembered today in Catholic circles in France for his work as the director of the Apostleship of Prayer in Le Mans through which he contributed to the spread of devotion to the Sacred Heart. On October 17, 1870 Fr de Boylesve was appointed to preach at the Visitation of Le Mans upon St. Margaret Mary for his subject, who at the time was a Blessed. He also preached upon another mystic who had died within their own times, Mother Marie de Jesus (1797-1854) from the convent des Oiseaux of Paris who had received revelations from the Sacred Heart that were favourably recognised by the Archbishop of Paris. On June 21, 1823 the Sacred Heart revealed to Sr. Marie that He desired France be consecrated to His Sacred Heart by the King, and that a chapel be built and dedicated to Him, and the feast of the national consecration be formally celebrated every year. "After my sermon," recounts Fr. Boylesve, "the Mother Superior expressed to me her astonishment at my silence with regard to an almost similar order that Our Lord had given to Blessed Margaret Mary on June 17th, 1689. I confessed that in our college, which had barely opened for a month, I had not found the letters of the Blessed One and that I was unaware of the apparition and the order she was telling me about. I promised to make good this omission." Apparently at that time, the Sacred Heart's requests to St. Margaret Mary for a shrine and the national consecration of France by the King were not yet widely known.

True to his word, filled with his characteristic zeal for faith and country, doing what he could to extend the reign of Jesus Christ through his beloved homeland and secure its safety, the very next day he repaired his omission by publishing a pamphlet featuring the prophecies of St. Margaret Mary and Mother Marie de Jesus entitled "Triumph of France by the Sacred Heart", composing a special prayer of consecration to be said, which the Zouaves said every Friday as hope in the Sacred Heart was sorely needed. Paris was threatened with destruction by bombardments, then starvation by the invading Prussians, having commenced a siege around the city in September 1870. The siege continued until January 1871, the citizens reduced to dire circumstances. The zoo animals were slaughtered for food, the populace also living off of stray animals and rats. While Prussian advance had ceased, humiliation still ensued when France suffered defeat at the hands of the Prussians with the establishment of the

German Empire, also losing the territory of the Alsace-Lorraine to the victors. The troubles were not over. From March to May 1871 Paris fell into the clutches of the anticlerical socialist Communards, rebels revolting against the new government of the Third Republic. Blood ran in the streets, historical buildings burned, including the Tuileries Palace. The anticlerical Communards also executed the Archbishop of Paris, Georges Darboy, fulfilling the prophecy of St. Catherine Laboure. This horrific turn of events, combined with the circulation of prophecies foretelling the destruction of Paris was at hand, the faithful no doubt felt doom hung over the city. The times were desperate. After several reprintings, including a full reproduction of the text by Fr. Ramiere in the 'Messenger' newsletter issued by the Apostleship of Prayer, more than 330,000 copies of Fr. de Boylesve's pamphlets of the 'Triumph of the Sacred Heart' were circulated. It contributed to the rapid spread devotion to the Sacred Heart and bolstered the call to have the Universal Church consecrated to the Sacred Heart, also to build a national shrine on Montmartre in atonement for the atrocities committed by the Communards who began their uprising there. Construction began in 1875, the cornerstone was laid on June 16, 1875, the day Bl. Pius IX encouraged all the faithful to pray the consecration to the Sacred Heart using the special formula composed by the Sacred Congregation of Rites for the 200th anniversary of the apparition of the Sacred Heart to St. Margaret Mary. The construction of Sacre Coeur was at last completed in 1914.

As for Fr. Boylesve, in addition to his efforts to spread devotion to the Sacred Heart he worked unceasingly at many other endeavours, not only as director of the Apostolate of Prayer in Le Mans, but also with the Confraternities of Saint Joseph such as that of the Good Death, and also the Confraternity of the Agonizing Heart, the Work of Campaigns, Conferences of St. Vincent de Paul, Workers' Circles, he still appeared to dare all and sundry that they would never be able to find enough work for him to do. He amazed all that he was never at a loss for a subject to preach upon. He could easily vary his sermons to where it appeared he never preached the same way twice, and always captured his hearers' attention. One day out of curiosity a hardened sinner walked in to listen to him preach and left a converted man. When Fr. Boylesve wasn't working, he was praying. There was no question that he maintained a deep spiritual life. He was transferred to Vaugirard in 1875, returning to Le Mans two years later in 1877. Three years later his teaching came to an end at the college there with the decree of March 29, 1880 issued by the French minister for public education prohibiting the Jesuits from engaging in their educational apostolate, only the first of several anticlerical laws that would be passed in France over the next decades. Fr. Boylesve admitted he was on the verge of tears saying his last Mass for the students in the chapel before the school closed. Yet, he remained as active as ever despite this terrible blow, preaching, giving catechisms and continuing his writing, tackling the problems of their day threatening both the Church and society.

As his mediation booklet of St. Michael was printed in 1882, this was one of his endeavours during this time to defend the Church and to fortify the courage of the faithful by spreading devotion to the saint. It is plain to see from the text Fr. de Boylesve was particularly devoted to this great archangel of Heaven, the Great Commander of the Heavenly Hosts who continues to burn with the same ardent zeal for the glory of God as when he thrust Lucifer and the other rebel angels out of Heaven so long ago. We see the knightly Fr. de Boylesve gives no quarter to the enemies of the Church in his text. In several instances of this booklet he does not hold back when pouncing on Freemasonry and castigates it in a bold militant tone. We must remember the infamous 'Alta Vendita' documents of the anti-religious Italian Carbonari lodge were already published in French in 1859 at the request of Bl. Pius IX and Leo XIII, revealing the insidious plans of the secret revolutionary societies to destabilise and undermine the papacy and the Church. No doubt the Risorgimento in Italy was seen to be one of the evil fruits of these dark plans when the last of the Papal States were defeated and the period of the 'Prisoner in the Vatican' pontificates began with Bl Pius IX in 1870. Fr. de Boylesve mentions this bleak period in this book of St. Michael. Also, the attacks against the religious orders in France were obviously seen by him as an extension of these subversive movements. To use a pugilistic expression, Fr. Marin apparently beat Pope Leo XIII to the punch in condemning Freemasonry: his booklet of St. Michael was printed two years before the pope's famous encyclical 'Humanum Genus' was published in 1884!

Fr. Marin continued working despite his old age, until the end of 1891 when his activity was curtailed. He was struck with various ailments, first a tormenting dermatitis that remained with him, then inflammation of the blood that restricted his activities for many weeks, although he managed to say Mass and continue his writing, until at last he was struck with paralysis, unable to walk or speak. Clutching his rosary and his crucifix, the ever zealous 'priest-knight' of the Vendée gave up his soul to God in February 22, 1892 and was buried in the Jesuit cemetery of Sainte-Croix.[1]

---

1   Biographical information from 'Necrologie. Le Père Marin de Boyleseve, in 'Lettres de Jersey', Vol. XII, No. 1 (April 1893)

Foreword

In great struggles nothing is done apart from the direction of the general-in-chief. It is in this sense that we believe we could apply to the Archangel Saint Michael certain traits where Scripture indicates the action of the angel of the Lord without naming him. Even when in these circumstances Saint Michael would not have acted in person, it is permissible to assume that being the leader of the heavenly militia, he is no stranger to the intervention of the spirit under whose orders he acts. The reader, moreover, cannot be misled, because we have taken care to propose the applications that we make to the Archangel Saint Michael as simple insinuations, authorized, it seems, by the example given by the Church herself in her liturgy.

Fr. Marin de Boylesve, S.J.

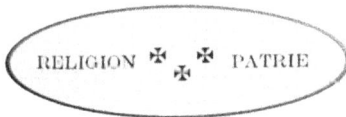

RELIGION ✠ ✠ PATRIE

Saint Michael According to the Bible

ഐ❖ൽ

First Day:
Michael and the Dragon

"And there was a great battle in heaven, Michael and his angels fought with the dragon, and the dragon fought and his angels." (Apoc. 12:7)

Lucifer, in the intoxication of his pride, cried out: I will be like the Most High; St. Michael replied: Who is like God? *Quis ut Deus?* And the fight started. Terrible struggle of which our most bitter battles are only a faint image, because the struggle between minds, the struggle between intelligences, the struggle between the wills surpasses the struggle between the corporal bodies and is all the difference that separates the material order and spiritual order. An obstinate struggle, a struggle henceforth eternal which will last as long as heaven, as long as hell. Lucifer and his own therefore persist in saying: I would be like the Most High; St. Michael and his own persist in repeating: Who is like God?

Finally an abyss opened, it was Hell; the

angel of light became the angel of darkness and tumbled to the bottom of this abyss, dragging down with him all the accomplices in the revolt. At the same instant Heaven opened, it was the Heaven of glory which succeeded the heaven of trial.[2] St. Michael and his own rushed towards the Thrice Holy God to contemplate Him face to face and to eternally enjoy the society of the Three Persons of the August Trinity.

Let us never leave off from affirming truth and denying error; victory is the reward of constancy. When the spirit of falsehood and evil persists in falsehood and evil, it only sinks deeper and deeper into the abyss of nothingness. The victory will therefore certainly remain with the defenders of truth and justice, provided they do not cede an iota. The slightest concession made to error is already an error; the slightest concession made to injustice is already an injustice.

ഇ❖ര

---

2   'The heaven of trial' - this refers to the empyrean Heaven where the angels were created outside the Heaven of the Blessed Trinity. The angels were created in this lesser Heaven where they could not have sight of the Blessed Trinity as it was necessary they be tested first to prove their faithfulness and therefore merit the Eternal Beatific Vision.   If they had seen the Blessed Trinity beforehand they would never have ceased to see or love God and therefore would have been beyond testing. God decreed they had to be tried first. See '*All About the Angels*' by Fr. Paul O'Sullivan, O.P., Ch. 5.

Second Day:
The Three Envoys and Abraham

"There appeared to him three men standing near him." (Gen. 18:2)

We can believe that these three men, or rather these three angels, appearing to the Patriarch in human form, represented the three persons of the Holy Trinity. Perhaps these three angels were also those whose names Scripture has given us: Michael, Gabriel, Raphael. Michael, who since the fall of Lucifer is the leader of the heavenly militias, would represent the Father; Gabriel, who will be the messenger of the Incarnation of the Word, would represent the Son; Raphael, whose name means Remedy of God and who was the guide of young Tobias, would represent the Holy Spirit who, through justification, gives souls supernatural life and who guides us in the ways of salvation.

The role of the Archangel Michael is to intervene especially in solemn circumstances. Now, was there ever a more solemn circumstance than this one where it was a question, first of promising the faithful Abraham the miraculous birth of a son from which the Saviour of the world was to descend, then of announcing a catastrophe which was to represent the terrible punishments reserved for criminal nations?

"Abraham and the Three Angels"

Perhaps it would also be possible to think that the one of the three angels who remained alone with Abraham was the Archangel Michael representing God the Father and speaking in His name. This interview, so simple and so familiar, shows us how mercy always mixes with justice, and teaches us that never forgetting His title of Father, God is always more ready to forgive than to punish. If there were only ten righteous in Sodom, that abominable city would not have perished.

Glorious Saint Michael, intercede again for the guilty nations! Present to God the innocent and the penitents, the men of prayer, the men of zeal and devotion; they are numerous enough to disarm His just anger. May you also find in my soul and in my life, enough good works to compensate for the sins which call upon me the blows of Divine Justice!

೫❖ಜ

"Abraham's Sacrifice" (1655)

Third Day:
The Angel and Isaac

"And behold an angel of the Lord from heaven called to him, saying: Abraham, Abraham. ... Lay not thy hand upon the boy." *(Gen. 22: 10-11)*

The Angel of the Lord stopped Abraham's arm already raised to sacrifice Isaac; but on the day of the sacrifice of Him of whom Isaac was only the figure, he did not come to stop the arm of the executioners. Why should we be more demanding when it comes to the Holy Church and especially ourselves? The Church is the mystical body of which Jesus is the Head; the body cannot be spared more than the Head; and if the Leader had to go through suffering and humiliation to enter into glory, if the cross was the standard of victory after having been that of combat for the Leader, the body must follow the Head. The Church must resemble Jesus, and for her as for Jesus, suffering and humiliation are the doors of glory. For her, as for Jesus, the cross is the sign of victory as well as the sign of rallying together.

Children of the Holy Church, brothers of Jesus, members of His Body under a Head crowned with thorns, following a crucified Head, we must not, we cannot escape the sacrifice; and it is not only in symbol, it is in reality that we must carry our daily cross and immolate ourselves on this cross

Often it is true God confines Himself to asking us to sacrifice the heart, and satisfied with our good will, at the moment when the real sacrifice was about to be accomplished, He sends His angel with orders to tell us: 'It is enough; the will shall be counted to you for the deed.' But there are sacrifices that must be consummated. It is that one above all, and it is not the least hard, which will ultimately be accomplished - it is the sacrifice of life. (The time of our death.)

At this solemn moment, come oh glorious St. Michael, come at the hour of this formidable combat which is called the agony (or combat) *par excellence*, come, not only to assist me in this decisive fight but to also receive my soul and then lead it to heaven.

ಹ ❖ ೞ

Fourth Day:
The Angel and Jacob

"And behold a man wrestled with him till morning." (Gen. 32: 24)

An angel who represents God Himself fights all night against Jacob: Jacob persists in retaining him until he has obtained along with his blessing the assurance of protection against Esau whose resentment he fears.

You are enveloped in a deep night, the future is unknown to you; yet you know only too well both the strength of your enemies, and your own weakness. You see no way to escape, no help at hand to overcome. Pray and persist in prayer: by prayer you will be strong against God Himself.[3]

---

3   Fr. Marin's reflection does not indicate we pray 'against' God, but rather we must pray with persistence despite all obstacles. If we preserve in prayer with faith, and if our requests are in accordance with His Will, God will relent and grant the graces we need and seek from Him similar to when the angel representing Our Lord finally relented in the face of Jacob's persistence and granted the favours he sought.

Esau's jealousy against Jacob is reminiscent of Satan's against man. In revenge for the preference through which our human nature has been the object of the Incarnation, Lucifer has resolved to have us lost. For this purpose he disguises himself sometimes as an angel of light, sometimes as a serpent. As angel of light, he seeks to communicate to us his pride and his spirit of revolt, not ceasing to whistle in our ears: 'You will be like gods', *eritis sicut dii*; as serpent, he arouses sensuality in us, never ceasing to raise the flesh against the spirit.

St. Michael has broken the pride of the rebellious angel, he has slain the old serpent and he holds it under his feet. Let us attach ourselves to the invincible Archangel and pray to him until he has assured us the victory.

ജ❖രു

"Jacob Wrestling with the Angel"

Fifth Day:
The Angel and Moses

"There appeared to him (Moses) in the desert of Mount Sinai, an angel in a flame of fire in a bush." (Acts 7:30)

Saint Stephen says that it was an angel who appeared to Moses in the burning bush. It had to be the angel of the people of God, the Archangel Michael whom St. Gabriel calls "the great prince who fights for the people of the children of Israel". (Daniel, 12, 1).

Like that fire which enveloped the bush and did not consume it, the glorious archangel lights up and sets ablaze; he lights up without dazzling, he sets ablaze without burning.

It is quite different with Lucifer. Since his fall he has only dazzled. He was the first to dazzle himself; in his pride he believed and told himself he was more than he was, and he wanted more than he could have: pride inspires only pride.

St. Michael on the contrary sheds light and truth with this humble and proud war cry: *Quis ut Deus?* Who is like unto God?

He reminds us that all greatness and all strength comes from God, from God without Whom we can do nothing, from God through Whom we can do everything.

Since his fall Lucifer has been consumed by the fire of jealousy and hatred, and imparting the dark ardour of envy which devours himself, he burns all the hearts he touches. Once upon a time he set the Pharisees ablaze with jealousy and hatred against Jesus; nowadays he sets the enemies of the Church ablaze, he envelops and penetrates their souls with a jealous hatred which consumes and devours them; and at the same time he divides good people, inspiring them with that odious jealousy which does not allow them to get along and unite together against the wicked.

But on his side, St. Michael envelops and sets fire to hearts a pure charity and the flames of a zeal that seeks only the glory of God and the salvation of souls. This heavenly ardour purifies without consuming; it dispels depraved affections and aversions, but without destroying the holy vivacities of the love of good and without extinguishing the noble indignations of the hatred of evil.

ಬಿ ❖ ಣ

Sixth Day:
The Angel and the Camp of Israel

"And the angel of God, who went before the camp of Israel, removing, went behind them." (Exodus: 14:19)

The children of Israel had barely left Egypt when Pharaoh repents for letting them go and hastens to pursue them. It didn't take long for him to reach them. And the Hebrews were caught between the sea which stopped them and the army of the persecutor which surrounded them. But then the angel who preceded them, enveloped in a pillar of cloud, came and placed himself between their camp and that of Pharaoh. Bright on the side of the Hebrews, dark on the side of the Egyptians, the column did not allow them to approach the children of God.

At this moment the Church, stopped in its march by the revolution of blood and fire that is represented the Red Sea, sees itself enveloped by all the forces of the earthly powers of which Egypt and Pharaoh were the symbol. Like Israel, the Christian people tremble and think they are lost. But the protective archangel of the Church seems to have interposed himself between her and the human powers. Standing like a pillar of cloud, he projects on the Church a light which reassures and which enlightens upright and pure intelligences. This light revives in us faith in the promises of Jesus Christ and the hope of a new victory. At the same time the Archangel spreads over the camp of the new Pharaohs a thick darkness which disturbs and disconcerts the most skilfully combined designs. A dreadful night weighs on their minds and they dare not take a step.

Soon, it is true, seeing that the Church quietly crosses the waves of the revolution and that she is on the point of escaping them, they will launch madly in pursuit. But the revolution, after allowing free passage to the children of God, will close in on the persecutors so proud, so powerful, so threatening, to roll them in the waves of all the popular furies[4] and to engulf them in the depths of the abyss.

What the glorious Archangel does for the whole Church, he does for each of the faithful who call on him for help. He enlightens us, he reassures us: he spreads darkness and terror over our persecutors.

ఌ ❖ ༅

---

4   I.e. Fr. Marin seems to say the persecutors will be engulfed by the very 'popular furies' or secular democratic revolutionary agitations that they themselves have raised up against the Church, in the end, getting caught up in their own turmoil.

Seventh Day:
The Angel and the People of God

"Behold I will send my angel, who shall go before thee, and keep thee in thy journey." *(Exodus 23: 20)*

The Archangel preceded Israel; he precedes the Church. He keeps it, he protects it during its journey through the centuries and the nations. In the same way also by the guardian angels who under high direction are charged to accompany each of the faithful, the supreme leader of the angelic militias directs each one in particular during the dedication of this life; he assists us at the last passage, he defends us against the last assaults of hell, and finally he introduces us to the place that God has prepared for us, he leads us to heaven. Respect him: *observe eum*, listen to his voice: *audi vocen ejus*; let us be careful not to despise his inspiration: *nec contemnendum putes*. If we sin, jealous as he is of the honour of God, he will not leave our faults unpunished: *Quia non dimittet cum peccaveris*. In his intelligence and in his heart, the victor over the rebellious angel always bears the name of the God whose glory he upheld: *et est nomen meum in illo*.[5]

---

5   This reflection is based on the continuation of the Scripture passage quoted for the Seventh Day: "Behold

I will send my angel ... Take notice of him, and hear his
voice, and do not think him one to be contemned: for
he will not forgive when thou hast sinned, and my
name is in him." (Exodus 23:21)

Let us hear his voice, I repeat, let us follow his secret warnings and God will make him the enemy of our enemies, and he will afflict those who afflict us; *Quia si audieris vocem ejus et feceris omnia quae loquor, inimicus ero inimicis tuis et affligam affligentes te.* The angel will exterminate all the vices and sins represented by the peoples who occupied Palestine at the time when Israel was preparing to take possession of them: *praecedetque te angelus meus and intoducet te ad Ammorrhaeunt and Hetaeum and Pherezaeum Chananaeumque and Hevae unt and Jebusaeum quos ego conteram.*[6]

࿐❖࿐

---

6   Reflection based on the passage: "But if thou wilt hear his voice, and do all that I speak, I will be an enemy to thy enemies, and will afflict them that afflict thee. And my angel shall go before thee, and shall bring thee in unto the Amorrhite, and the Hethite, and the Pherezite, and the Chanaanite, and the Hevite, and the Jebusite, whom I will destroy. " (Exodus 23: 22-23).

Eighth Day:
The Angel and Mount Sinai

"This is he (Moses) that was in the church in the wilderness, with the angel who spoke to him on mount Sinai." (Acts 7: 38)

We are permitted to think that even today, guardian angel of the Universal Church, the Archangel Michael is in continual relation with the head of the new people of God to assist him in the government of souls, (I.e. the pope). At the same time, by means of the guardian angels of which he is the leader, he enlightens, he guides, he protects each of the simple faithful.

Do you want to hear the angelic voice, live on the heights, rise above the sounds of this world, above the currents of opinion, above the storms of passions, above the promises and threats of human power, above the hopes and fears of the world? Then like Moses you will hear the precepts of the law and understand them. Engraved on stone, nothing will be able to erase them from your memory or rather from your heart: filled like Moses with a holy zeal for the honour of God, you will overthrow the golden calf, you will break it and you will reduce it to dust. The golden calf is passion, it is vice, it is pleasure, it is greed, it is pride. Go up to Sinai every morning by prayer and meditation on the law of God; converse with the angel of the Lord, and when you descend into the valley, when you reappear among men, you will overthrow the idols that the flesh and the world would like to substitute for the true God.

ജ❖ര

Ninth Day:
The Prince of God's Army

"I am prince of the host of the Lord, and now I am come." (Joshua 5:14)

Joshua making a reconnaissance in the neighbourhood of Jericho suddenly saw himself in the presence of a warrior who stood up holding a sword in his hand. Without being disconcerted the leader of the people of God comes forward and asks the unknown one: 'Are you one of us or enemies?' - 'No,' the warrior answers, 'but I am the leader of the army of God, and now I come.' - Here more than ever, it is I believe, permitted to recognize here the Archangel Michael. - To this answer, Joshua prostrates himself to adore the representative of the God of hosts, and addressing the angel he said to him:

"Joshua and the Angel" (1860)

'What are the orders that the Lord intends to his servant?' 'Take off your shoes,' replied the angel, 'for the place you occupy is holy.' - Joshua obeyed. But what orders did the captain of the armies of Heaven give to the captain of the armies of Israel? Scripture doesn't say. We can suppose that Joshua received from the angel the indication of the course he was to follow in order to seize Jericho.

Jericho represents the world; follow the inspirations of your angel: before you the powers of the world will collapse as the walls of Jericho collapsed to the sound of the sacred trumpets, in the presence of the holy Ark. Be constant in prayer, unite together through religious manifestations,[7] through frequent Communions; repeat and resound aloud the words of Jesus Christ, the truths of faith, the teachings of the Gospel, the decisions of the Church: then all human forces, all the menaces of the ungodly will be in vain against you; and like Joshua, under the leadership of the angel, you will fly from victory to victory.

ഔ ❖ ന

---

7   I.e. as in public manifestations of our Faith, such as frequenting the Sacraments, attending Benedictions, processions and other public devotional services, etc.

Tenth Day:
The Angel and the Weepers

"And an angel of the Lord went up from Galgal to the place of weepers." (Judges 2:1)

By dint of fighting and victories, the children of Israel finally managed to settle in the Promised Land. But through either negligence or self-interest they spared a large number of the ancient inhabitants: yet these peoples belonged to a race cursed for their crimes and God had ordered them to be exterminated. The Angel of the Lord, probably the Angel of Israel, was sent to reproach them for this prevarication. 'You have treatied', says the heavenly messenger, 'with the inhabitants of these countries, this alliance will be fatal to you; you have not broken down the altars of their false gods, these gods will be your ruin.' The people then burst into tears; it was too late. God forgave them no doubt, but He declared to them through His messenger that the peoples they had spared would henceforth remain among them, that they would be to them like thorns in their eyes, like spears in their flanks, and that for many years they would force them to be kept on their guard continually and would often have to take up arms to free themselves. (See. Judges 2: 20-23)[8]

Our guardian angel warns us without ceasing to flee all dealings with the impious and the libertine, to completely exterminate all around us all the enemies of the faith and of the Divine Law. This is not about the extermination of people; what concerns us, we must not suffer in the sphere of our domain and in the circle of our influence a word that is said against God or that a work is done there against the Law. This is where our law and our duty end, but duty and law go that far.

Now what are we doing? After a few victories, we stop, we rest, we disarm, we conclude a tacit truce with our own passions and with the enemies of God. Soon the passions are revealed, the impious, the libertines rise up and take advantage of our unconcern, of our drowsiness, of our indulgence, they grow stronger and multiply as if to infinity. Soon the passions, the impious, the libertine make use of the freedom that we had the imprudence and the weakness to leave them, they hasten to take away from us the freedom to do well, and they end up reducing us to bondage.

So, at least let's open our eyes, finally

----

8   "And the wrath of the Lord was kindled against Israel, and he said: Behold this nation hath made void my covenant, which I had made with their fathers, and hath despised to hearken to my voice: I also will not destroy the nations which Josue left, when he died: That through them I may try Israel, whether they will keep the way of the Lord, and walk in it, as their fathers kept it, or not." (Judges 2: 20-23)

understand and recognize our folly, weep for our neglect; let us call to our aid the valiant and invincible Archangel Michael, let us pray to him to raise up strong and generous men who devote themselves to giving us the freedom to serve God, and let us begin by ourselves by exterminating vice and sin in our own hearts first, then in the sphere of our influence.

ജ❖ൽ

Eleventh Day:
The Angel and Gideon

"And an angel of the Lord came, and sat under an oak." (Judges 6: 11)

The children of Israel were groaning under the yoke of Midian. Then came the angel of the Lord and he sat under an oak tree located in the land of Ephra and belonging to Joash, head of the Ezri family. This Joash had a son named Gideon who was preparing to flee to the mountains no doubt to escape the domination of the invaders. It was to this young man that the angel appeared, saying: 'The Lord is with you, O most courageous of men, go in your strength and you will deliver Israel from the hand of Midian: know that it is I who you send.'

'The Angel Appearing to Gideon' (1561)

We know how with three hundred brave men Gideon delivered Israel.

Today impiety places the yoke of a learned and formidable tyranny on the children of God. And we ask where are the liberators? Strength and numbers are at the service of persecution. No human hope shines on the horizon. All that remains, they say, is to resign ourselves and to suffer.

That's not how Gideon reasoned. Rather than buying the rest of a quiet life at the cost of cowardly servitude, he prepared to seek freedom in the harsh life of the mountains and the desert. It was to this independent and generous man that God sent the angel of Israel.

Do not count enemies or friends; however large the number of some, however small the number of others; take your side, separate yourself from the crowd, withdraw into solitude. If the Lord is with you, what does the number matter? Thirty thousand men, ten thousand men against more than one hundred and twenty thousand, that is still much; but when God is with you, when God sends His angel to you, when the head of the heavenly militias fights with you, three hundred warriors are stronger than a hundred thousand, weakness becomes strength and numbers do not count.

჻

Twelfth Day:
The Angel and Samson

"Why askest thou my name, which is wonderful?" (Judges: 13: 18)

An angel appears to the wife of an Israelite named Manue, and he announces to her that she will have a son who will be consecrated to the Lord. Manue asks the heavenly envoy what his name is, but the angel refuses to make himself known and is content to answer that his name is admirable. It could well be the Archangel Michael here again. It is indeed to him that it is appropriate to announce the birth of this strong man, of this Samson who alone was to exterminate so great a number of Philistines! In this respect Samson recalls the glorious archangel who alone first dared to protest against the insolence of Lucifer, and who by this holy and generous boldness gave himself a name made to excite admiration forever: *nomen quod est mirable.*

Usually the strong men that God raises up against the oppressors of his people rise up alone, but soon around them we see elite warriors grouped, and it is only then that they march against the enemy. Samson will be alone all his life, and his whole life will be a struggle against the Philistines.

Among the men whom God raises up for the salvation of souls, there are also some whose mission is to fight and to act alone. But we cannot repeat it too often: God is with the one who devotes himself and sacrifices himself for glory and for the salvation of souls. Courage and confidence: if men abandon you, if the very ones whom you want to save give you up to the enemy as the children of Israel did to Samson, God will send an angel and, if necessary, the supreme leader of the angelic militia to escort you and to defend you.

Perhaps also through your fault, you will deserve to be abandoned by God Himself and to be reduced to your personal weakness. Even then, hope again: God will forgive you and restore your strength, and like Samson you will overcome even in death.

However, the memory of this strong man's weaknesses should serve as a lesson to you. Learn to free yourself from the senses through a pure and angelic life, and with the glorious Archangel Michael you will always be invincible and always victorious.

ജ ❖ ര

Thirteenth Day:
The Angel and David

"And when the angel of the Lord had stretched out his hand over Jerusalem."
(2 Kings: 24: 16)

To punish the vanity which drove David to count his subjects, God strikes the people with the plague of pestilence; but soon lets Himself be touched by the repentance and the tears of the holy king, and the angel is ordered to withdraw the hand which he had stretched out over Jerusalem.

It is often to punish the faults of superiors and especially priests that God allows plague, I mean licentiousness and impiety, to corrupt and destroy peoples. Now, who is it, who in a more or less extended sphere, has not exercised a fatal influence? At least let us weep for the souls that we have lost by our words or by our examples; let us weep for those whom we could and should have saved and whom through negligence and recklessness we have abandoned to their unhappy fate.

The angel's mission is not just to protect and defend; his function is also to execute the decrees of Divine Justice with regard to us. But whether he protects or punishes, it is always for the greater good of souls. If he protects, it is to ensure salvation; if he strikes, it is to turn us away from sin or to make us atone for it. The angel of heaven always offers to save us, in contrast to the angel of hell who always seeks to have us lost.[9]

෨ ❖ ෬

---

9   To explain Fr. Marin's reflection here, according to 1 Chronicles 21 Satan tempted King David to have a census taken of the people of Israel. Not that census-taking is necessarily evil, the Holy Family complied with the census that brought them to Bethlehem, but in David's case it was a matter of pride in human strength. Census-taking at the time was used for military drafts, (we see military men were numbered in the cesus of David), and also to determine taxes. In all, it was to evaluate the worldy strength and wealth of the kingdom. We observe a lack of trust in God here as military numbers mean nothing as indicated in the earlier reflection of Gideon defeating the enemies of Israel with only three hundred men because God was with him. David was therefore judging the kingdom according to human thinking regarding strength in numbers and not placing his trust in God.

Also, it has been noted he possibly was counting the people as his own possession and testing God. God promised Abraham his descendants would be as numberless as the sands of the seashore and the stars in the sky—it is for God to know the number, not man. Therefore it was not for David to number them, and, this census might be considered as putting God to the test to see if He had kept His promise.

Then we see God also allowed the whole nation to be punished for his sin as it states in 2 Kings 24:1 "And the anger of the Lord was again kindled against Israel", which is written before we read of King David taking the census. The Scriptures state we are

punished by what we sin by, "That they might know that by what things a man sinneth, by the same also he is tormented." (Wis. 11:17) It is possible the people of Israel were also becoming prideful in a worldly sense about the nation's growing numbers under David's kingship rather than reflecting that the success of the kingdom was due to God and His grace, and as a result God punished the entire people through its leader by permitting Satan to stir up David into taking the sinful census. The punishment also matched the sin, for David was given a choice of chastisement and agreed that allowing himself to fall into the hands of God was better than falling into the hands of men. He chose the punishment of three day's pestilence, which killed 70,000 thereby reducing the numbers of the populace he wanted to count. God, however, saw the repentance of King David, allowed His Mercy to be touched, and ordered the angel to withdraw his hand from Jerusalem.

In the reflection above, Fr. Marin then concentrates on how bad example leads people astray. In particular, those in positions of leadership and authority, especially priests and religious who are duty-bound to give good example for the salvation of souls entrusted to their care. We are also called to give good example lest we too lead others astray or cause scandal.

Fourteenth Day:
The Angel and Eliseus (Elisha)

"For there are more with us than with them." (4 Kings 6:16)

The soldiers of the king of Syria surrounded the city where the prophet Elisha lived. At this sight his servant is seized with fear. The man of God reassures him. 'Fear not,' he said to him, 'those who are with us are more numerous than our enemies.' And at the same time he begged the Lord to open the eyes of this man. Then he, (the servant) saw around Elisha an army of horsemen and chariots of fire. This was obviously the angelic hosts commanded or sent by the Archangel Michael to defend the prophet.

The infernal legions visibly represented by the earthly powers have surrounded the Church, and more specifically the Pope. There is not a man of God who, in the day of the power of the wicked, is not besieged and overcome by the soldiers and servants of the prince of the world. At this sight fear seizes us. Let us pray, let us open our eyes in faith, we will be fully reassured. Saint Michael with his angels hovers over the Church to protect her, and over impiety to reduce it to impotence; he surrounds the head of the Church and each of the men of zeal who fight the battles of the Lord; he wards off the blows of the enemy, he thwarts the perfidious plots of the adversary, he assures victory to those who, forgetting themselves think only of the interests of God, have placed all their trust in the all-powerful goodness of the Sovereign Lord of all things.

ഔ✤ര

Fifteenth Day:
The Angels and Isaiah

"And they cried one to another, and said: Holy, holy, holy, the Lord God of hosts." (Isaiah 6:3)

A great vision unfolds before Isaiah's eyes. The Lord appears to him seated on a throne shining with light. Thousands and thousands of seraphim never stop repeating: 'Holy, holy, holy is the God of hosts.' Archangel Michael is not named in the vision, but it is possible to think that in this immense concert his great voice dominates all the angelic chants. - However, it seems that the time is not well chosen to celebrate the glory and the power of the God of hosts, for at that time the world was even more corrupt than it is today.

63

Likewise today, as I write these lines, we would be more inclined to sing the *Miserere* than to sing the *Te Deum*. Well! Let us repeat one and the other. Let us implore heavenly mercy for those who are persecuted and for those who persecute; but above all let us exalt the power and the majesty of a God who never showed Himself more truly and more effectively the Lord of hosts. Never, in fact, was persecution more bitter, more universal, more skilful; the Church and religion were never more abandoned. Where are their defenders? And what are they? Freemasonry holds all the powers of the earth under its control. Fear chains voices and commands silence. Only a few devout faithful, a few priests, a few determined religious persist in fighting against impiety. And it is through these men so weak and so few that the Church continues its work. The mere fact of its existence in the midst of so many enemies conjured up to annihilate it would already be a miracle of the first order. What then of the miracle of its action, of its influence, of its power increasing, growing, multiplying with the storm and by the storm? Divine assistance was never more manifest. So let's sing with the angelic militias: 'Holy, holy holy is the Lord God of hosts!' - Blessed is also the leader of the heavenly armies, the glorious and invincible Archangel Michael who, today more than ever, can repeat his war cry; *Quis ut Deus*. Who is like unto God?

ഔ❖ര

Sixteenth Day:
The Angel and Sennacherib

"And the angel of the Lord went out, and slew in the camp of the Assyrians a hundred and eighty-five thousand." (Isaiah 37:36)

The impiety of Sennacherib was to mock the God of Israel. Camped in front of Jerusalem with an immense army, he believed himself assured of victory. It is true that the holy King Ezechias refuses to surrender; but recognizing his powerlessness in the presence of such a formidable enemy, he shuts himself up within his capital.

Today the number is against us. Impiety has the hundred votes of the press and millions of votes of universal suffrage. Let us humbly acknowledge our helplessness. However, let's not give in. Let us persist in resistance, but let us shut ourselves up in His Church and in the Heart of Jesus.

Ezechias put his trust in God alone; prostrate in the temple he shed his tears and his prayers before the Lord. For several months this confidence seemed little justified and little encouraged; prayers seem useless and in vain. The holy king always hopes and does not surrender.

Therefore God will finally show Himself. In a single night, in the twinkling of an eye, the angel of the Lord smites to death one hundred and eighty-five thousand warriors in the camp of the Assyrian king. And the proud Sennacherib runs away in shame with the wreckage of his invincible army. At this great blow we can recognize the angel of Israel, the glorious Michael.

Let us pray and resist: it is not enough to pray, it is necessary to resist, even if only by protestation by word, if one is reduced to the impossibility of acting: this is what Ezechias did by so doing, a noble response to the insulting challenges and insolent threats of Sennacherib. - It is not enough to resist and fight, we must pray, and like the pious king of Judah, we must pray with invincible confidence. These two things together, prayer and resistance ensure Divine help, and if a miracle is needed, God will do it. He will send His angel and the ungodly will be exterminated.

ജ❖ൽ

'Destruction of the Army of Sennacherib'

Seventeenth Day:
The Angels and the Captivity in Babylon

"And behold Michael, one of the chief princes, came to help me." (Daniel 10:13)

In the struggle which the Archangel Gabriel had to sustain against the angel of the Persians and against that of the Greeks, he found only the Archangel Michael to assist him.[10]

---

10   In this reflection Fr. Marin explains how the angel Gabriel came to the prophet Daniel, to bring comfort and explain to him the vision he had seen, but the angel first declares why he was delayed in helping him – that the 'Prince of the kingdom of the Persians', had delayed him twenty-one days, but that prince Michael came to his aid. St. Gabriel also admits he will have to struggle against the prince of the Greeks too, and his only helper will be St. Michael. Fr. Marin of course is correct in proposing that it must be the guardian angels of the Persian and Greek nations who blocked St. Gabriel, as only an angelic prince could impede another, and that it took another angelic prince to help him. Also, we see no other prince would come to St. Gabriel's aid except St. Michael, which means he asked his fellow angels for help, but did not receive it. Why? Since the good angels cannot sin, this resistance cannot have been caused by sinful motives. Fr. Marin explains they had holy desires to help their respective peoples by keeping the Jews near them so that they might learn the ways of the One, True God, and used their influence to keep the Jewish people near, but St. Gabriel and St. Michael knew this resistance could not be allowed to continue - if the Jews stayed too long in a pagan country, they were in danger of losing their

Knowing that his people were to succeed the Assyrians in the domination of Asia, the angel of the Persians sought to prolong the stay of the children of Israel in the empire of Babylon. He hoped that their example and their words could gradually bring the Persians to the knowledge of the true God. The angel of the Greeks also endeavoured to delay the return of the Hebrews to Judea, in the belief that their presence would be useful to his people, when in their turn they invaded the East. Foreseeing the influence of the Romans on almost all the nations of the world, the angels of the pagan peoples undoubtedly supported those of the Persians and Greeks to obtain the extension of the stay of the Hebrews in the middle of this empire that the Romans were to invade after the Greeks. The glory of God and the salvation of souls were therefore the motive of their efforts.

But the Archangel Gabriel judged, not without reason, that the dealings of the infidels compromised the faith and the customs of the Jews; he feared that, if the dispersion continued, (i.e. the Babylonian captivity), this people would also come to forget the true God instead of making Him known. Now Gabriel is particularly interested in maintaining the faith in the nation from which the Messiah is to emerge, from

---

faith. However, according to Fr. Marin's reflection, God permitted the 'holy struggle' between the angels as He was pleased to see them zealous for His glory and for the spiritual welfare of the nations entrusted to their care.

whom he has predicted His coming, death and reign. For his part, Michael is especially the angel of the people of God, he will be the angel of the Church, and consequently of the great human family as a whole. He therefore united with Gabriel to hasten the restoration of the Jewish people. In his eyes, the special interest of this small people merges with the general interest of humanity and outweighs the more immediate interest of the peoples who must receive the influence of the Persians and Greeks. Finally, Michael's intervention will prove Gabriel right.

God, however, is pleased with a struggle for which glory and the salvation of souls are the sole motive. If there is any difference in the views of these blessed spirits, it is because, enlightened as they are, they do not yet know the last word of the secret and of the Divine plan.

So let us neither be surprised nor scandalized if sometimes there arises among the men of God some disagreement on the best means to be taken to glorify God and to save souls. When on both sides we have in view only the honour of God, it is permissible to seek to make prevail the plan which we believe to be the wisest, provided that on both sides we observe the respect demanded by charity, provided that we recognize and respect the righteousness of the intentions of those who, although differing with us in opinion on the choice of means, nevertheless propose the same goal, the glory of God and the salvation of our neighbours.

"Holy Trinity with Saint Michael
Conquering the Dragon" (1666)

Eighteenth Day:
The Angel and the Man of Sin

"At that time shall Michael rise up, the great prince, who standeth for the children of thy people." (Daniel 12: 1)

At that time, in the time of the triumph of the man of sin, (the Antichrist), when everything will seem hopeless and the persecution will be pursued to the point that nothing like it has never been seen, then the leader of the angelic militia will rise. So do not tremble! Your opponents are powerful, numerous, formidable, threatening, triumphant! A little more, it appears all over with the Church, with religion! - Rest assured, St. Michael is more powerful than all those powerful on earth. He is the grand prince, *princeps magnus*, and to speak the language of contemporary politics, he is the great power.

The activity of the ungodly is frightening. It looks like a fire, it looks like the fire of hell; under the burning breath of Lucifer all the institutions, all the religious works are devoured by the flame and collapse in a vast blaze - Do not fear. Archangel Michael has his eye on them and on you. He is watching, he is standing: *qui stat pro filiis populi sui,* he is ready to defend the sons of his people. At the moment willed by God, he will rise up, and he will break up the little contemporary antichrists, as he once broke Lucifer, as one day he will break the formidable Antichrist at the end of time, as he has already broken all the oppressors from the Cains, the Pharaohs, the Balthasars, the Anitochuses, the Neros, the Julians, the Ariuses, the Luthers, the Voltaires, the Robespierres, up to those who we are not yet allowed to name.

ಏ❖ಞ

Nineteenth Day:
The Angel and the Profaner

"For there appeared to them a horse with a terrible rider upon him." (2 Mach. 3:25)

Heliodorus advances towards the temple of God; he prepares to carry out the orders he has received from his master king. He lay hands on the treasures devoted to divine worship and on the gold entrusted to the faithful priests. The people tremble and pray. The high priest Onias, powerless against force, has no hope except in God. Suddenly a rider appears mounted on a war horse. Heliodorus is knocked down by the courier and trampled underfoot, then severely flogged by two young warriors who escorted the

"Heliodorus cast from the Temple"

formidable rider. St. Michael's intervention can be assumed here.

Iniquity is on the verge of being consummated, impiety triumphs; this is the end of the Church's treasures, of her material goods and above all of her spiritual goods. Christian children are going to be taken from their families and from the Church, which is their spiritual family, to be delivered up to godlessness.[11] Invoke the glorious Archangel, entrust him with the temples, religious buildings, Catholic institutions, the priesthood and Christian childhood. The new Heliodoruses will be so badly flogged that they will not risk returning.

ॐ❖ॐ

Twentieth Day:
The Angels and Judas Machabeus (Maccabeus)

"When they were in the heat of the engagement there appeared to the enemies from heaven five men." (2 Mach 10:29)

---

11   This is an obvious reflection of Fr. Marin's time when the anti-clerical French state seized more control over Church property and Catholic schools, plus the erosion of parental rights with public school education, further promoting the dictates of the government enforcing the separation of Church and State.

Mounted on battle horses with gold bridles, they went before the army of the Jews. Two of these horsemen escorted Judas Machabeus, they protected him with their weapons and they deflected all blows from him, while they rained on the enemies a hail of bolts accompanied by lightning flashes which, blinding them, sowed among them disorder and confusion thus toppling them over each other. We may well think that the leader of the angelic militias was no stranger to this protection with which Heaven surrounded the hero of Israel.

The Jews fought for their faith and for their law; they defended their religion and their country against a persecuting tyrant. God assisted their zeal with a miraculous intervention.

Let us defend religion and virtue against the impious and against the libertines. Let us dare everything for God, let us forget ourselves, let us devote ourselves: then we will be allowed to count on the extraordinary assistance of the angels of heaven; and their leader, the glorious St. Michael, will assure us victory.

☙ ❖ ❧

'Agony in the Garden' c. (1680–1719)

Twenty-First Day:
The Angel and Jesus in Agony

"And there appeared to him an angel from heaven, strengthening Him." (Luke 22:43)

Pious authors believe that the Archangel Gabriel was specially attached to the person of Mary. We may well assume that the honour of serving Jesus during the course of His earthly life fell by right to the supreme leader of the angelic militias, and that it was he who received from the Heavenly Father the commission to assist the Saviour at the time of the dreadful agony.[12] But what then was the angel's mission? It was not to remove the chalice from the lips of the Divine Agonising One that he was sent; it was not to console Him in His immense desolation; it was to fortify Him in combat and in suffering. What an example! What a lesson! He who is strength itself accepts the help of an angel! We, therefore, who are weakness itself, are permitted to implore the help of the angels when the trial exceeds the ordinary measure.

Let us address ourselves mainly to the head of the blessed spirits. He will perhaps not

---

12   In the section 'The Angel and the Agony' in 'St. Michael According to Tradition' Fr. Marin shows why it is believed by some pious authors St. Michael was the angel that came to Our Lord in Gethsemane.

deliver us from the evils that we dread or which already seem to overwhelm us, but he will rekindle our courage in us, he will give support to our patience, he will strengthen our countenance, and finally for us, as for Jesus, the crown of he thorns will be turned into a crown of glory, and the chalice of sorrow will become the chalice of eternal sweetness.

ଛ❖ଔ

Twenty-Second Day: The Angel and the Risen Jesus

"For an angel of the Lord descended from heaven." (Matt. 28:2)

The body of Jesus rested in the tomb under the vigilant guard of the soldiers that the princes of the priests had taken the sagacious precaution to place in front of this monument of their triumph. But now the earth quakes. The enormous stone which closed the sepulchre is overturned and on this stone an angel is tranquilly seated. This angel's gaze shone like lightning, his garment as white as snow. At this sight, the soldiers fall half-dead with fright and they only get up to run away as quickly as possible. But the angel reassures the pious

80

'The Resurrection'

women who come to the tomb to once again render Jesus the customary honours of burial. "You," he said to them, "fear not; for I know that you are looking for Jesus who was crucified: He is no longer here: He is risen according to His word: come and see the place where the Lord was laid. Hurry, go, tell His disciples that He is risen. He will precede you to Galilee, there you will see Him, as I have foretold to you."

Even when all would seem lost, even when crucified again in His mystical body which is the Church, and in its members who are its priests and faithful, Jesus would seem locked in a tomb and asleep in death, we shall still hope, and, as soon as it comes to a matter of His service and His honour, let us go, speak, act. It is then that the head of the heavenly armies will show himself, here, thundering upon the enemies of Jesus and of the Church in the very midst of their triumph, and there, consoling those generous souls who will not have been afraid to exert themselves to give honour and to serve Jesus suffering in His priests and in His persecuted faithful.[13]

ജ❖ൽ

---

13   In the section 'The Angel of the Resurrection' in 'St. Michael According to Tradition' Fr. Marin shows that the archangel is indeed believed to have been the angel at the tomb, which explains why he included this Gospel in this monthly devotion to St. Michael.

Twenty-Third Day:
The Angel and the Apostles

"But an angel of the Lord by night opening the doors of the prison, and leading them out, said: Go, and standing speak in the temple to the people all the words of this life." (Acts 5:19-20)

The prince of the priests and his dignitary assessors had the apostles arrested and locked them up in public prison; but during the night the angel of the Lord opens the doors of the dungeon, brings out the apostles and says to them: 'Then go to the temple and announce there to the people the words of life.'

The wicked have you expelled, they have closed your temples, they have thrown you into prison: God seems deaf to your complaints and your prayers. One might even say that He closed His eyes to the triumph of your enemies who, however, are your enemies only because they are His; it seems that He does not see the evils which fall on you only because you devote yourself to His service. Also the night of desolation envelops you, and you sleep the sleep of despondency and sorrow. Know, however, that God does not forget you. Suddenly the prison doors will open and you will be free. The angel of the Church will set you free. For you, priests and religious, the temples and the establishments will reopen, you will resume the course of your teaching there and you will not stop announcing the doctrine of salvation there: *Stantes loquimini in templo plebi omina verba vitae hujus.* (Standing speak in the temple to the people all the words of this life.)

ഔ✤ൖ

Twenty-Fourth Day: The Angel and St. Peter

"And behold an angel of the Lord stood by him." (Acts 12:7)

Peter is in prison: the Church continues to pray for his deliverance. Tomorrow, Herod will sacrifice him to the wrath of the Jews. It is night. Tied by a double chain, Peter sleeps peacefully between two soldiers. Guards keep watch in front of the prison door. This look like the Popes of the present century: Pius VI, Pius VII, Pius IX, Leo XIII. Herod still holds Peter in bonds, because it pleases the enemies of Jesus Christ: *videns quia placeret Judaeis.* ("And seeing that it pleased the Jews" - Acts 12: 3) Only one word would need to be changed, instead of the Jews read: Freemasons.

But here is the angel of the Lord; the dungeon lights up; the angel touches the apostle and wakes him up, saying to him: "Get up quickly." The chains immediately fall from the hands of the prisoner. - "Sit down and put on your shoes," adds the angel; Peter obeys - "Take your garment", continues the heavenly envoy, "and follow me." - Peter follows him. He thought he was dreaming. However, under the guidance of the angel, he passes through all the walls of the prison. The iron door opens in front of them, they walk down the street, and the angel disappears. It was only then that Peter recognized that he was really out of prison. "I know now," he said to himself, "that the Lord has sent His angel and has delivered me out of Herod's hand and the expectation of the Jews."

When it comes to the deliverance of the Church, it is difficult not to believe in the intervention of one who is the patron and special angel of the new people of God as he was of the old. It was in 1870, September 20: to please the Revolution a new Herod blocked up the Head of the Church in the Vatican as in a prison. Night came. It has been long. As we draw these lines here it is eleven years since it has lasted.[14] All

---

14   Fr Marin is referring to the bleak period of Church history during the Risorgimento when the last of the Papal States were defeated. The period of the

mighty here below, impiety is preparing to put an end to the Pope, with the priesthood, with the Church, with religion. Within this thick darkness which envelops the whole world, everything is asleep. Peter himself sleeps in the prison. It is impossible to see the slightest glimmer of hope.

Let us pray, however, and pray tirelessly. Suddenly, in the very midst of this dark and gloomy night, just as the tyrants are about to strike the decisive blow, the angel of the Lord will thwart the plans of ungodliness, and the persecutor will be precipitated into blood and in mire.

He was proud, the persecutor Herod, under his royal garments and on his tribunal when he harangued the people. In hearing him the crowd cried out: *"Dei voces et non hominis."* ("It is the voice of a god, and not of a man." Acts 12:22) But this cry, this universal clamour was the signal for the fall. The angel of the Lord struck the royal orator; and suddenly the persecutor of the Church, devoured by worms, died in torment. - Take care: the Pope, the priest, the religious are sacred people. Do not touch them!

စာ✤ကာ

'Prisoner in the Vatican' pontificates began, starting with Bl Pius IX in 1870 and ending during the reign of Pius XI when the Lateran Treaty was signed in 1929 recognising Vatican City as an independent city-state.

Twenty-Fifth Day:
St. Michael and the Devil

"When Michael the archangel, disputing with the devil, contended about the body of Moses." (Jude 9)

The Devil undoubtedly wanted to discover the body of Moses, in the hope of pushing the people of Israel towards rendering an idolatrous cult to the great man who had delivered them from the bondage of Egypt. St. Michael fights against the Demon to keep the body of the man of God in obscurity. However, great as he is, the glorious archangel simply presents himself as the envoy of the Lord; to overcome the Devil and to reduce him, he speaks only by the name of God. "The Lord Himself commands you," he said to the infernal spirit: *Imperet tibi Dominus.*

Let us learn from this example not to rely on our own strength, and to fight only in the Name and by the orders of God. Let us also learn to seek obscurity, and let us be careful not to attribute to our own virtue the glory of the great things that God has been able to accomplish through our ministry. Our honour, moreover, will not suffer. If the sepulchre of Moses has remained unknown, his name has remained glorious.

જ❖ભ

"St. Michael and the Angels Taking the body of Moses"

"The Angel of the Apocalypse Appearing to St. John"

Twenty-Sixth Day:
The Angel and the Sealed Book

"And I saw a strong angel, proclaiming with a loud voice: Who is worthy to open the book, and to loose the seals thereof?" (Apoc. 5:2)

The Heavenly Father, seated on a throne, holds in His right hand a book written inside and out and sealed with seven seals. A mighty and strong angel raising his voice cries out: 'Who is it that is worthy to open the book and break the seals?' Wouldn't it be here again the Archangel Michael repeating in another form: *Quis ut Deus*? Who is like God? And declaring by this new challenge that only the Incarnate Word is worthy of opening the book which contains the destinies of the world?

Yes, He alone, the Lamb who was slain for the salvation of men, He alone, this Lamb who is also the Lion of Judah, is strong enough to open the Divine book, powerful enough to carry out the judgements that justice and mercy wrote there together.

Do you want to triumph with the Lion of Judah on the Last Day, then stand under the standard of the Lamb here below. This standard is the Cross. The Church, in its liturgy gives to Saint Michael the title of standard-bearer (*Missa pro defunctis*).

Following the glorious archangel, declare yourself loudly for the Cross.

Could it not be the same archangel who suspends the action of the four angels charged with punishing the earth, and retains them until all the chosen ones are marked on the forehead with the sign of the living God: *Et vidi alterum angelum ascendeniem ab ortu solis, habentem signum Dei vivi.* (Apoc. 7: 2) "And I saw another angel coming up on the east side, having the sign of the living God, and he cried with all your might, to the four angels who were given power to harm the earth and to the sea, saying, Do no harm until we have marked the servants of our God on the forehead." Is it not for the standard bearer of the Lamb of Calvary that he is above all to mark the chosen ones with the sign of the Cross?

When we make upon ourselves this sign of salvation, of victory and of life, let us pray to the glorious Gonfaloniere, the Standard-Bearer of the King of Kings to inspire us with his courage and to communicate his strength to us.

ಐ ❖ ಛ

Twenty-Seventh Day:
The Angel and the Censer

"And another angel came, and stood before the altar, having a golden censer." (Apoc. 8:3)

In the liturgical office, the Church authorizes us to recognize the Archangel Michael in the person of the angel who appears after the opening of the seventh seal, at that solemn moment when seven angels each received a trumpet to successively give the signal of the last plagues. This angel holds a golden censer and he receives the prayers of the saints to offer them to God as an incense of pleasant odour. *(Cfr. Offci. S. Michaëlis I noct., Ant 3)*

Here everything is symbolic. The gold of which the censer is made represents the purity and charity which give to prayer its value and its effectiveness. The incense which is consumed while burning represents the spirit of sacrifice which must accompany prayer, so that, united with the sacrifice of the Divine Lamb, it rises towards God the Father, all impregnated with the vapour of the Blood of Jesus.

Let us entrust our desires and our wishes to the Archangel Michael. Presented by him, they will be purified and sanctified.

Twenty-Eighth Day:
The Angel and the End of Time

"And I saw another mighty angel come down from heaven." (Apoc. 10: 1- 11)

Of the seven angels who were to announce by the sound of the trumpet the plagues of Divine Justice, six have already given the dreadful signal. But before the last plague God grants a pause. A mighty angel descends from heaven. He is covered with a cloud: a rainbow shines around his head; his face is dazzling like the sun; his legs look like pillars of fire. In his hand he holds an open book. He puts his right foot on the sea and his left foot on the earth. His voice is that of the roaring lion. He cries and seven thunders respond to him. Raising his hand towards the sky, and calling as witness the One who lives for ever and ever and Who created heaven, the earth, the sea and all that is contained therein, he swears that there will be no more time: *quia tempus non erit amplius.*

This extraordinary angel who appears to be leading the great fight against Lucifer and who seems to be like the prime minister of the Almighty Lord, could still be the Archangel Michael. In this immense drama of which the Apocalypse is the picture, the leader of the celestial legions must reappear at all solemn moments.

He is holding an open book in his hand. Let us join the apostle Saint John in requesting this book. It is the book of truth, it is the book of righteousness. Read it, meditate on it, devour it. It will fill us with an interior bitterness, with a holy and vigorous indignation against the enemies of God, against the seducers who corrupt souls by the perfidy of their speech and their teaching. Therefore, to obey the order of the angel, we engage against impostors and impious blasphemers with the battle of the word, without fearing their threats and their violence: *Oportet te iterum prophetare gentibus et populis et linguis et regibus multis* . ("Thou must prophesy again to many nations, and peoples, and tongues, and kings." Rev. 10:11)

ൟ❖ൠ

"Woman clothed with Sun -
St. Michael Casting Down the Dragon"

Twenty-Ninth Day:
Once Again St. Michael and the Dragon

"And there was a great battle in heaven, Michael and his angels fought with the dragon." (Apoc. 12:7-9)

It is always the great combat which has begun in the heaven of trial[15] which, continuing during the series of centuries, takes formidable proportions at the end of time. Already struck down, Lucifer and his angels were thrown from the height of the heavens to the depths of hell; stripped of their glory, they were clothed with the hideous and terrible figure of the serpent.

The fight is currently engaged against the Church, represented by a Woman who also figures the Mother of the Saviour and whom the Dragon pursues with anger: *Iratus est Draco in mulierem.* ('And the dragon was angry against the woman.' Apoc. 12:17)

Let us not flatter ourselves that we are escaping a fight in which we are the prize at stake. Rest for us is impossible in the midst of a battle in which the actors are competing precisely for our soul, some will us to lose it, others to save it. Let us therefore join the army of angels, and under the leadership of the

---

15 I.e. the empyrean Heaven. See the footnote for the First Day meditation.

Archangel Michael, we will defeat the Dragon and the Beast of which he is the inspiration, and the false lamb which he uses to deceive and to seduce.

It would be necessary here to meditate on these admirable chapters of the Apocalypse (13-16) where all the artifices of the Dragon and all the movements of the heavenly host are described. Under the supreme direction of their leader, the angels succeed one after another to ensure the victory of the elect and to complete the defeat of the old serpent. Finally, it is all over with the empire of Babylon, a figure of the world and of power, it is all over with the empire of the Beast, which represents the sensual impiety at the end of time. Woe to those who have become intoxicated with the wine of unclean Babylon and have allowed themselves to be marked with the seal of the Beast. Here an angel descends from heaven with great power; the light of his glory illuminates the earth and with a great voice dominating over the crash of the empires which unfolds, he cries: *Cecidit, cesidit Babylon illa magna*; Babylon the great is fallen, is fallen (Apoc.. 18: 1-2). The hour of vengeance has come. Standing on Mount Zion, the true Lamb, surrounded by all who have His Name and that of His Father written on their foreheads, leads the combat and ensures the victory of St. Michael and all the faithful angels.

We live in troubled times which are already resembling the last moments of the world and which one could take for the preludes to the agony of a dying man. Let us not tremble. If the action of the Dragon and the Beast is visible and manifest, while that of St. Michael and his angels appears to be more hidden, it is not any less real despite seeming hidden. The power of darkness has its hour, but it is only an hour; the day of triumph will soon dawn for us, and this day calls for eternity.

ଔ❖ଓ

Thirtieth Day: The Angel in the Sun

"And I saw an angel standing in the sun." *(Apoc. 9:17)*

Heaven showed an angel to the eyes of the Apostle; out comes a white horse ridden by a Rider who calls Himself the Faithful, the True, and Who judges and fights with justice. His eyes shine like flames; on His head He wears several diadems, His garment is sprinkled with blood. He is called the Word of God. He is followed by all the armies of heaven whose warriors also ride white horses and are dressed in white and pure linen. From His mouth issues a two-edged sword; on His garment and on His side it is written: 'King of kings and Lord of lords'. Then an angel appears in the sun and with a powerful voice announces the defeat of the Beast and the kings of the earth who had united to fight against the sublime and formidable Rider. Couldn't we say these are the powers of the present century who joined forces with Freemasonry to exterminate the Church of Jesus Christ?

What is this sun in which this angel appears, if not the One who is the Sun of Truth and of Justice? We know that Scripture goes on to multiply the symbols which represent Him and which recall Him.

Then an angel, who could well be the same one who earlier appeared in the sun, descends from heaven holding the key to the abyss and an immense chain to bind the Dragon, the ancient serpent who is the Devil and Satan (Apoc. 20: 1-2); but here the mystery becomes more and more impenetrable. No one yet has been able to explain with any certainty[16] what is to be

16   One might dare say this is not quite true, which is somewhat surprising considering Fr. Marin's extensive learning. Fr. Marin must have been unaware that along with St. Augustine the Church has generally declared the thousand years mentioned in Ch. 20 of the Apocalypse is to be regarded as a symbolic number representing the last age of time starting from when Christ shed His Blood on the Cross and established His Church and ending with His Second Coming at the Last Day. Therefore, the number is not to be taken literally according to the Church. (See the footnotes to the Douay-Rheims Bible regarding the thousand years.) Attempts to make literal interpretations of the thousand years have often led to the heresies of Chiliasm and Millenarianism and their heretical variants that have been condemned by the Church.

understood by this reign of the righteous for a thousand years and by this supreme effort of Satan unleashed at the end of this millennium to be finally thrown into the lake of fire and sulphur where the Beast and the false prophet will be tormented day and night for ever and ever.

What we know at least is that this great fight, which began with the victory of St. Michael over Lucifer, ended as it began, with a solemn and definitive triumph of the glorious Archangel over the enemies of the Incarnate Word of which he was the first worshipper.

Under the leadership of the invincible leader of the angelic legions, let us fight until the end. Victory is assured. "Behold He comes", *Ecce venio cito*, says the One who is the Alpha and the Omega, and I bring with Me the reward to render to each one according to his works. I, Jesus, I send My angel to announce the arrival of My triumph. *Ego, Jesus, misi angelum meum, testificari vobis haec in Ecclesiis*. (Apoc.. 22:12, 16, cf. Ibid., V. 6 and 8). Come therefore, Lord Jesus, *Veni, Domine Jesus*. (Apoc. 22:20)

ℬ ❖ ℭ

CONCLUSION

O, glorious St. Michael, come to the aid of God's people: *Veni in adjutorium populo Dei* (Offic.) Thou who are the leader of paradise, to whom all angels pay honours due to this high rank: *Michaël praepositus paradisi, quem honorificant angelorum vives;* thou who have appeared in the presence of God all shining with glory, and whom the Lord has clothed with a marvellous splendour: *Gloriosus apparuisti in conspectu Domini, propterea decorem induit te Dominus;* thou who art God's messenger for righteous souls; *Dei nuntius pro animabus justis*; and who received the incense to burn before the golden altar that rises before the eyes of the Lord: *Data sunt ei incensa multa, ut adoleret ea ante altare aureum, quod est ante oculos Domini*: thou of whom countless wonders are told because thy strength in battle has determined the victory: *Multa magnalia de Michaële archangelo, qui fortis in praelio fecit victoriam*; thou whom God has established as prince over all the souls whom thou must gather for heaven: *Constitui te principem super omnes animas suscipiendas*; glorious prince, St. Michael the Archangel, remember us, at all places and all times, pray for us before the Son of God: *Princeps gloriosissime, Michaël archangele, esto memor nostri: hic et ubique semper precare pro nobis Filium Dei*. **Amen.**

Saint Michael According to Tradition

ജ❖ൠ

Saint Michael in the Arts

Christian art has recounted in its language all the phases of the struggle that Saint Michael and his angels sustained from the beginning at the foot of the Eternal throne. But the leader of the rebel legions was not wiped out in his challenge. He is still alive, and his angry cry has not ceased to resound since the day of his revolt. He is the genius of evil. For his part, the prince of the heavenly militia is still the defender of the rights of God. He is the antagonist of Satan. It is this thought that painting, sculpture, poetry, music have expressed in a thousand different forms.

Saint Michael has almost always the physiognomy of an adolescent who has lost none of the graces of youth and possesses all the strength, all the wisdom of middle age. A few 15th century pilgrim clichés shows him with the beard and features of an old warrior, but such examples are rare for Christian iconography. The beautiful face of the archangel is calm and the passions have never altered it; however he is serious, even a little severe, his gaze, accustomed to seeing God face to face, retains the limpidity of crystal, but he is vigilant, he observes the enemy. Such must be the angel of battles. St. Raphael, the friend of the travelling man, is the type of goodness; joy suits St. Gabriel, the ambassador of God to Mary; the attitude of a warrior distinguishes Saint Michael.

What costume should be given to this mysterious soldier, whose nature is quite celestial, whose strength is entirely divine?[17] A tunic, a shield, a spear. This has been understood by artists who were inspired by the sources of the purest traditions. Saint Michael received from God a mission analogous to that of the priest, and we prefer to see him dressed in the white tunic of the Levite than in the heavy armour of the combatant; he affirms and he defends the truth: but he does not take the initiative to attack, his shield and spear are sufficient for him to keep his enemy at a distance and repel his poisoned features. Among the most notable types in this genre are a miniature from a 10th century psalter belonging to the British Museum, a coloured line drawing from the 11th century kept in the Avranches library, a miniature from an *Apocalypse* from the 14th century that is part of the Firmin-Didot collection.

---

17   I.e. as coming from the Divine. All of St. Michael's angelic power and strength comes from the Divine power of God. French pious authors, such as St. Louis-Marie de Montfort, are known to use 'divine' in this manner. (E.A. Bucc.)

Sometimes the spear is replaced by an arrow. There is an example of this in a statue from the 7th century, placed on the portal of the cathedral of Cortona. As early as the 13th century, a number of miniatures or pen drawings depict the Archangel with a helmet on his head and a sword in his hand. We find proof of this in a manuscript from Mont-Saint-Michel transported to Avranches at the time of the Revolution. Finally around the middle of the 14th century and especially the 15th, the full armour of the knight replaces the old costume, or rather fantasy becomes the sole rule of the artists, and the prince of the celestial militia is decked out in the most bizarre outfits. We would not be able to recognize him without his wings always outstretched for the action, without the monster slain at his feet. How more beautiful, more poetic he was under the simple garment that the true friends of Christian art had given him!

Lucifer himself did not escape mutilation. This infernal serpent, this terrible dragon, which the holy books describe to us in the darkest colours, has become with time a vulgar robber, hardly worthy of attracting the attention of the least of men.

In truth, we could make to several artists this reproach that Dom Hugues addressed to the pilgrims of the 12th century:

"There are those who imagine, who when they immediately hear about the escutcheon and dagger of Saint Michael, that they are told that this archangel chased the Devil from paradise with his weapons. But these are chimeras in their minds. Because who does not know that the combat which was made in heaven between the good and the bad angels is seen not by the clanking of the weapons but by the disunity and dissension of their wills? " (*General history of the abbey of Mont-Saint-Michel.*) (*Annales du Mont-Saint-Michel, June 1881*).

ఴ❖ఞ

The Angel and the Agony

"Jacob was returning to Mesopotamia, and fearing for himself and his family on account of the old hatred of his brother Esau, he crossed a torrent which blocked the way, then divided his house into two bands and remained alone to recommend it to God. This is a figure of Jesus dividing His apostles into two groups to pray alone and Who continues in prayer. While Jacob, in fact, was praying for his family and his posterity, behold an angel in human form comes to reassure him of his personal blessings; but he assures him that of his descendants, that the

Synagogue cannot be blessed; that, on the contrary, it was to be cursed and annihilated, since one day it was to deny and kill the Messiah."

"At the news of the future fate of his people, Jacob shuddered with horror. He takes the angel body to body, grasps him and does not stop wrestling with him all night long, declaring that he will not release him until he has obtained the promise that the Jewish people, although guilty of deicide, will nevertheless be preserved and will one day receive His pardon and blessing; as far as he obtains, finally, to be thus the same Jacob blessed in the person of his posterity and of his people. *Non dimittam te nisi benedixeris mihi.* " (VENTURA, 6th conf. *On the Passion.*)

"This fight can be seen as a figure of the agony of Jesus in the garden. But who was this angel who came from heaven to earth to console the Divine Agonizing One? Michael is the leader of the angelic militia, the great adversary of Satan and the prince of the Synagogue of whom Jesus was the most worthy Person; Was it not then up to him to strengthen God made man in the supreme combat where He reversed the empire of Satan, where the Synagogue was granted the glory and the facility to transform into the Christian Church." (BLOT, *Agony of Jesus*)

This is the opinion of Denis le Chartreux, Mansi, Meffreth, Marie of Agréda and in particular of Saint Bonaventure, whose story is voiced.

While the Lord Jesus prays in the midst of the most terrible anguish, there the angel of the Lord, Michael, the prince of the heavenly militia, stands at His side, strengthens Him and speaks to Him in these terms: "Jesus, my God, I greet you. I presented Your prayer and Your sweat of blood to Your Father in the presence of all the heavenly court. Prostrated before His Divine Majesty, we all begged Him to remove this chalice from You. The Eternal Father replied: "Jesus, My beloved Son, knows that the Redemption of mankind which in this form is the object of Our desire, cannot take place without the shedding of His Blood which is of an infinite price; and therefore, if He wants the salvation of souls, He must die for them." "Lord, what do You choose?" Then the Lord Jesus answered the angel: "I want with an absolute will the salvation of souls: I therefore prefer to die and that they be saved, these souls that My Father had created in His image, rather than not die and not redeem them. May My Father's will be fulfilled!" "Courage then," the angel told Him, "the works of the Son of the Most High must be magnificent and His courage invincible. The pains will pass away quickly, and their rigours will be succeeded with immortal glory. Your Father tells You through my mouth. He is always with You, He watches over Your mother and Your disciples: He will return them to You safe and sound." The Lord receives with respect and humility these words of encouragement even from His creature, for He considers Himself a little below the angels, while He is in this sad valley of darkness. (St. Bonav. *Med*. T. I, c. LXXV)

The Angel of the Resurrection

On the dawn of the first day of the week the Gospel tells us Mary Magdalene and the other Mary came to the sepulchre. At that moment there was a great earthquake. For the angel of the Lord descended from heaven, approached the sepulchre, rolled the stone which closed the entrance and sat on it. His face was shining like lightning, his clothes were white as snow. The terror with which he struck the guards was so great that they were as if dead. However, the angel said to the women: "For you, fear not; I know you are looking for Jesus who was crucified. He is not here; for He is risen as He said: come and see the place where the Lord was laid. Then hurry to go and tell His disciples that He is risen; and behold, He is going before you into Galilee; there you will see Him, as I told you." (Matt. 28)

We find here all the traits of grandeur common to the apparitions of Saint Michael. The terrible and glorious apparatus with which he is surrounded, the terror which he inspires in the

guards posted around the sepulchre due to the hatred of the Jews, the importance of the mystery which he comes to announce to the world, the exceptional circumstances in which God through him manifest His glory.

Because of their dignity, the people of Israel had been committed to the care of Saint Michael; the holy archangel is in charge of the new family of the Saviour, of which he becomes the guardian angel.[18]   It is on this Easter day that he comes to take possession of his new office.   The apparatus with which he is surrounded reminds us of his fiery sword in the earthly paradise, the thunder and lightning of Sinai. As he descends from Heaven, the sea stirs, the earth trembles.[19]

But if this earthquake terrifies the guards posted near the sepulchre due to the hatred of the Jews, [20] the archangel reassures the holy women, announces to them the resurrection of Jesus Christ, and through them to the apostles and to the Church.

Saint Michael collects on this day the reward of his generous initiative in his fight against Satan. He becomes the minister of Him

18   Original footnote: Michael fuit praepositus Synagogae, sed ex quo Synagoga crucifixit Christum, translatus est nobis ad praeposituram et custodiam. (S. Bern., Sant.)
19   Original footnote: Concussum est mare et contremuit terra, ubi archangelus Michael descendebat de coelo. (Off. S. Mich.)
20   Original footnote: Viso terrae motu et his quae fiebant timerunt valde.

whose person he worshipped in advance, humbled in the infirmity of the flesh. Christ entrusts to him the care of the Church, his Bride, the Sovereign Pontiff His vicar, and when France will take its place in the sun of truth, when it becomes the Eldest Daughter of the Church, Saint Michael will be the angel of our fatherland. (*Annals of Mont-Saint-Michel*)

ജ❖ഝ

The Feast Day of St. Michael

In 493, under the Pontificate of Pope Gelasius I the glorious archangel appeared on Mount Gargano, now Sant'Angelo, in the Kingdom of Naples. The lessons of the Breviary recount the fact:

"A priest, looking for a bull that had strayed from his flock, found him with his horns caught in a cave. As an arrow shot at the animal to force it to retreat, the arrow turned against the one who had shot it. This extraordinary fact filled with such fear those who had witnessed it, that henceforth no one dared approach the cavern. The bishop of Siponto was consulted, he ordered three days of prayers, after which the archangel Saint Michael himself declared that this place was under his protection, and to which

"The Legend of Mt. Gargano"

he had wished to indicate, by the fact which had kept them in suspense, the worship that was to be rendered to the Lord in this place, as well as to him and to all the holy angels. The bishop at once went with his people to the cave, which he found built in the form of a church, and there he celebrated the divine services. The place later became illustrious by several miracles."

"In recognition of the benefits that the Messenger of the Almighty brings to the Church, a feast is established in memory of this event and in honour of St. Michael. Since the 5th century, it has been celebrated on the 29th of September. This holiday was afterwards held most solemnly in several Western countries.

"Here is what we read in the ecclesiastical laws published in 1014 by Ethelred, King of England:

'Let every Christian of the prescribed age fast for three days with bread and water, eating only uncooked rations before the feast of St. Michael, and let every man go to confession and to the church barefoot... . Let each priest go three days barefoot, in procession with his people; that each one prepares what he will need for food for three days, observing, however, that he has nothing fat and that everything is distributed to the poor; that every servant be dispensed from work during these three days to better celebrate the feast, or that he do only what is necessary for its use. These three days are the Monday, Tuesday and Wednesday before St. Michael's Day. '

Additional note about the Apparitions of Mt. Gargano: Traditional sources say it was a rich landowner who went looking for the bull. The traditional account says the bull was found kneeling at the entrance to the cave and refused to budge, hence the owner angrily shot an arrow at it to try and get it to move, which miraculously was shot back at him. Also, the words of St. Michael to the Bishop of Siponto are as follows:

You have done well to ask God what was hidden from men. A miracle that struck the man with his own arrow, so that it was clear that all this happens by my will. I am the Archangel Michael and I am always in the presence of God. The cave is sacred to me. There will be no more shedding of bull's blood. And since I have decided to protect this place and its inhabitants on Earth, I wanted to attest in this way that I am of this place and of everything that takes place as patron and custodian. Where the rock is thrown open, the sins of men can be forgiven. What will be asked here in prayer will be granted. Go therefore to the mountain and dedicate the cave to Christian worship."

It has been suggested that the place was once an ancient pagan shrine dedicated to the god Mythras that once was honoured by bull sacrifices during secretive rites held in underground temples and caverns, hence the declaration of St. Michael that bull's blood would no longer be shed at the site. Some accounts then say the Bishop thought he had dreamed the vision and ignored it until several years later when the diocese was threatened with invasion. St. Michael appeared again and promised the city would be spared if the citizens attacked the enemy with faith, no doubt with confidence that he would aid them. This happened, but the bishop still did not consecrate the site or build a church. The next year he decided to appeal to the Pope for counsel on the matter and the Holy Father ordered three more days of prayers and fasting before the cave, however, it is said the bishop still had not ventured into the cave. St. Michael appeared to him again, and this time declared to the bishop he need not consecrate the cave as he himself had done it. The bishop and his entourage discovered an altar had been erected that was covered with a deep red altar cloth, the altar surmounted by a Cross. Tradition also states St. Michael left his footprint in the rock, affirming his presence and his consecration of the place. It is the only building of worship in the Catholic Church that has not been consecrated by man and has therefore been given the name the 'Celestial Basilica'. St. Francis of Assisi deemed the place so holy he remained at the entrance and dared not enter as he considered himself unworthy to set foot in the place consecrated by the great Archangel. While September 29 is indeed the official feast day of St. Michael, his appearance on Mt. Gargano is also celebrated on May 8.

While on the subject of Mt Gargano, it would be remiss not to include the famous fourth apparition of 1656. A plague was ravaging the countryside, and Archbishop Giovanni Alfonso Puccinelli made a special appeal to St. Michael. The townspeople composed a special prayer to the Archangel imploring his aid, which the archbishop and placed in the hands of the statue at the shrine of Mt. Gargano. The archbishop received a miraculous reply on September 22 at his palace when on that morning during his prayers he heard a mighty sound resembling an earthquake, followed by a flash of light. St. Michael appeared before him and commanded him to bless stones from the holy cave and inscribe a cross and the letters 'MA' on them for 'Michael the Archangel'. The great prince assured him that anyone who had a stone and kept it with devotion would be preserved from illness and receive his protection. The bishop did as requested and those who had a blessed stone were cured of the plague. Since then 'relic stones of St. Michael' can be obtained from the holy shrine. Exorcists have also noted that in their ministry they are helpful powerful sacramentals that curb the power of the devils. (E.A. Bucc.)

ജ❖ൽ

St. Michael and France

Saint Michael is the first patron of France. It was Queen Clotilde who put the homeland of our fathers, in a very special way, under the protection of this powerful archangel.

The famous Mont-Saint-Michel abbey, so aptly called the Wonder of the West, was founded in the 7th century.

It was Saint Aubert, twelfth bishop of Avranches, who, after three apparitions of Saint Michael, built a magnificent church in 708 in honour of the holy archangel. The huge and picturesque rock once called the Tombe or In Peril of the Sea was then no longer known by any other name but Mont Saint-Michel.

The many miracles which took place at this sanctuary, through the intercession of the holy

Mont Saint-Michel

archangel, spread everywhere his fame and made his pilgrimage famous not only in France but throughout Christendom. People came from all over Europe, although they did not then have the easy means of communication that we have nowadays. Charlemagne and after him almost all the kings of France went there. It was there that the Illustrious Order of the Knights of Saint Michael was established in 1469; and until 1789 the pilgrims came there in crowds, to beg the great archangel to obtain for them strength and patience in their troubles, firmness and courage when dangers threaten the fatherland. (*Liturgical week of Poitiers.*)

Additional Note: Tradition states that St. Aubert was afraid he was a victim of an illusion or dream, and hence delayed fulfilling St. Michael request to have a shrine built in his honour. Some accounts say he was also procrastinating as he dreaded the difficulties that would entail building such a shrine on the mount, which at the time was surrounded by pagan druid settlements, which could also pose a problem. Finally, during the third vision, St. Michael placed his flaming finger on the head of the procrastinating monk and burned a mark that went to his skull, this proving he was not under any delusion and that this request was not to be deferred. Today the saint's skull may been seen in the Cathedral of Saint-Gervais d'Avranches. The hole said to have been made by St. Michael is visible.

Other miracles connected with Mount Saint-Michel or 'Mount Tomb' are recounted in the 'Life of St. Michael' in the 'Golden Legend' by Jacobus Voragine (1275), translated by William Caxton, 1483 as follows. St. Aubert also wondered where the location of the monastery should be placed, and St. Michael told him the site would be where thieves had hidden two bulls, (which he obviously found). He wasn't sure of the size of the site, but the angel told him the breadth would be the size of the bulls steps, and hence the site was discovered through a sign with bulls involved, as in Mt. Gargano. One of the workers then found two huge rocks that were impossible to move, but he saw St. Michael who told him to move them, and this time they were as light as a feather.   Then, when the church was built, St. Michael brought a piece of marble on which he stood, along with a piece of cloth brought from his other shrine, (apparently from Mt. Gargano). As the site was lacking water, the angel told them to make a hole in the marble, and water gushed forth. (E.A. Bucc.)

ಏ❖ಚ

The Shells of St. Michael

The faithful who in the past centuries went on pilgrimage to the famous sanctuary of Mont Saint-Michel each began to take away a fragment of the miraculous rock dedicated to the glorious archangel. As the competition was immense, immense also their pious damage would have lasted, if a severe law had not been passed from the first days against any visitor who would have allowed himself to detach a stone from the holy mountain. As for this law, no one dared to break it; for, in addition to active surveillance, the archangel followed those with his anger who carried off a few pieces of the granite after succeeding in deceiving the guardians. It was said that despite the defences a pilgrim from Italy had taken a small stone from the rock to put it in the altar of the church of a monastery near his home. But God allowed him to be afflicted with a strange disease against which care and science were equally powerless. He did not obtain his healing until he brought back to the Mount the stone he had stolen from it.

But then what relics could now be offered to the pilgrim who often come from far away? Should he therefore, against all odds, bring back as the only souvenir his emotion and the tears shed at the feet of the archangel? In the middle of the sands covered twice a day by the waves of the rising tide, the blessed rock seems to be able to offer only the rock itself. However, Saint Michael provided.

> "Nature is so good that it has sown in the shifting arena of sand a resource more abundant than the manna of the desert. It is this (scallop) shell with deep radiant furrows, with plump valves as if washed with a pale crimson colour. A small cylindrical hole, the only vestige of life that the waves have respected in retreating, indicate the former habitation of the organism. From there it ascends to the surface of the Ocean, the poor little animal, on one of its scales erected as a row boat, and under the other one manoeuvring like a sail. There is there also the mark of the finger of God, as in all of nature." (Ch. Nodier.)

The first pilgrims must have recalled that the humble shells had been reddened by the blood of the martyrs, when in the past the bruised and bloody limbs of Christ's first confessors had been thrown on their broken points.[21] The latter pilgrims then, with a holy

---

21   Original footnote: "In their barbarism the persecutors strewed the floors of the dungeons with

eagerness, seized the shells to touch them to the miraculous rock and to have them blessed in the sanctuary of the archangel; and so consecrated by this blessing, they became, so to speak, relics themselves.

The shells have been for them what in other places were the coral pearls which had been strewn in the hair of our first virgins. They made necklaces with them, and on each shell, as on each bead of a rosary, the pilgrim sang a prayer in honour of the archangel as he went along his way. Soon a necklace was not enough, the pilgrim covered himself wholly with shells, and then there came families rushing upon the Mount who had no other means of living other than to collect the shells and sell them to the pious visitors. This is how in the middle of the

---

broken shells, and on this bed they rolled the shattered bodies of the martyrs." (Additional Note: There are accounts regarding the early martyrs in Rome that a number of Christians were tortured by having their flesh scraped from the bone by ragged shells, while others were tormented by being forcibly stretched out on broken pieces of shells. In latter times, the French Jesuit missionary to New France, St. Isaac Jogues (1607-1646), had his thumb cut off with a scallop shell, only one of the many tortures he endured. While St. James the Greater is the saint most closely associated with the scallop shell, this is not a symbolism of his martyrdom. When his body was discovered it was found covered with scallop shells, hence the shell became a symbol of the pilgrims travelling the Camino to his shrine at Compostella. We also see from the account above the scallop shell became associated with pilgrims visiting Mont Saint-Michel as well. - E.A. Bucc.)

French lead pilgrim badge
St. Michael slaying the dragon

(c. 14th to 16th century)

9th century, when fleeing from the Normans, the women of Avranches came to earn their daily bread.

Then they made artificial shells out of lead; and for this purpose, in the 11th century a foundry was established at Mont Saint-Michel. Simple at first, the shell then featured the effigy of the archangel. He was shown with outstretched wings, his head surmounted by a helmet, his right hand armed with a cross, the left with a shield, and, under his feet, lay vanquished the enemy of God and of men.[22]

From then on, the shell was part of the history of Mont Saint-Michel: we are going to see it playing a big role. It will no longer be a symbol for just the pilgrim, it will also be for the abbey, it will be for the knights, it will be for the kings who will do the honour to wear it. Not only has it become the terror of Satan, but it will become the terror of the enemies of France, Eldest Daughter of the Church, of France that was solemnly consecrated to the Archangel.

---

22   Original footnote.: "Some of these shells have been found; they date from before the 13th century. We also find, on the date of February 15, 1393, letters patent of King Charles VI, granting rights of aid in favour of those who sold them." (Additional Note: Of interest, excavations were conducted on part of the Mount where a storm had caused damage in 1999. Archaeologists discovered several of the stone moulds once used to make these lead pilgrim badges and souvenirs dating from the 14th and 15th centuries. The moulds depicted scenes of Saint Michael, the Virgin Mary, the traditional scallop shell, and pilgrim's trumpets. E.A. Bucc.)

In 1420, Robert de Jolivet[23] placed it on the shield of the abbey, which was six shells of sable (black). There we see what had become of the the shell, and yet its role was not finished. When Louis XI instituted a military order of valiant knights "in honour of Saint Michael, first knight of the Good Lord, who armed himself for his quarrel against the enemy of the human lineage, and was thrown from heaven."[24] He gave for adornment to his brave members the pilgrim's adornment, which had already become that of the abbey. Their necklaces were gold entwined with shells;[25] their long coats, lined with ermines and embroidered with gold were bedecked with silver shells; and the arms of the order were: ten shells of Saint Michael of sable (black) with a head azure (blue) with three fleur de lis gold.

And the kings of France, their great masters, were the first to deck the shell on their person. Thus it was both the emblem of the pilgrim and that of the knight, and if we compare it to the sacred sign of our redemption, similar to the cross of Jesus that the virgin takes to wear on her breast with honour and the captain armed with a sword for the defence of his country, it

23   Robert Jolivet (d. 1444) was a Norman Benedictine and the thirty-first abbot of Mont Saint-Michel from 1410-1444. (E.A. Bucc.)

24   Original footnote: "Words from the decree of Louis XI."

25   From 1469 to 1516 the necklace of the Ordre de Saint-Michel featured twelve golden shells strung together with knotted laces. (E.A. Bucc.)

Front and reverse sides of a gold badge of the French Royal Order of St- Michel. Badges with shells were reputedly presented to ecclesiastic members, whose numbers had grown to one hundred before they were reduced to six by decree of Louis XIV in 1655 as part of a reform of the chivalric order.

became the symbol of bravery while remaining the symbol of prayer, without which bravery could not exist.

And now in our days we have seen reborn the shells of the pilgrims and knights of yesteryear; we again see the crowds; and with them the traditional emblem; may we also see more and more the visible effects of the protection of the Archangel Saint Michael, patron of the Church and of France, its Eldest Daughter! (Borrowed from the *Semaine du Fidéle*)

෨ ✤ ෬

St. Michael and Charlemagne

"In the midst of his victories, Charlemagne never lost sight of the conquests of the kingdom of Jesus Christ, the expansion of which he had more at heart than that of the States. He had omitted nothing to bring about the conversion of the idolatrous Saxons. But the frequent revolts of these restless peoples disturbed and halted the progress of the faith. As soon as they saw this prince occupied in the Italian war against King Didier, they entered the lands of the Franks, setting fire everywhere and particularly in holy places, in hatred of religion. A detachment went to burn the church of Fritzlar. It was Saint Boniface who had it built, and he predicted that it would never be burned. These idolaters made every effort to set fire to it; but the Christians who were in the fort, and the pagans of the Saxon army, saw two young men dressed in white who were defending this church.[26] The Saxons were so terrified that they fled without anyone pursuing them. Near the church was found a dead Saxon who was kneeling, holding in his hand fire and wood, and in the posture of a man in the act of puffing to light a fire. " (Rohrbacher, *Hist. De l'Église, IX.*)

છ❖ભ

---

26   According to some accounts the two men who appeared by Divine Intervention also rode white horses. Fr. Marin obviously assumed St. Michael must have been one of the heavenly white warriors that intervened which accounts for his quotation of this text here since it is known St. Boniface was greatly devoted to the archangel and in a special way entrusted his missionary efforts to him. One time St. Boniface encountered tremendous difficulty while attempting to eradicate a pagan temple and convert the heathens in Bavaria, he was about to give up until St. Michael appeared in the sky in the act of defeating the dragon. (E.A. Bucc.)

St. Michael and St. Joan of Arc

Under Charles VII the protective angel of France appeared to Joan of Arc and told her "that God had great pity on France; that she must go to the aid of the king: that she would raise the siege of Orleans, and deliver Charles from his enemies." Joan having answered that she was only a poor girl incapable of leading an army, the heavenly envoy added that Saint Catherine and Saint Marguerite would come to visit her, that they had been chosen to guide her and assist her with their advice. He himself taught that he was the Archangel Saint Michael. - "I saw him," she said to the judges, "with my bodily eyes, as well as I see you." - Not content with this extraordinary help, Saint Michael appeared visibly and stopped the enemy on the Orléans bridge. Indeed, after the attack on the entrenchment of Belle-Croix, the English prisoners told later that they seemed, at that moment, to be surrounded by a multitude of assailants, and that they had seen in the air youths of dazzling beauty mounted on white horses; the Archangel Michael himself had appeared to them marching across the bridge at the head of the French.[27] Also Charles VII had

---

27   There are stories that that not only was St. Michael seen riding on a mount in the sky, but also the patron saint of Orléans, St. Aignan. The account attributed to an English prisoner tells of a sudden appearance of 'troops', the English were given a strange impression

the image of the glorious archangel painted on his flags, with these two mottoes taken from the prophet Daniel (10:13, 21) *"And behold Michael, one of the chief princes, came to help me. ... And none is my helper in all these things, but Michael your prince. "*

St. Joan also had a special banner, and "she had it made just as Saint Catherine and Saint Margaret had shown it to her, saying to her: 'Take this banner in the name of the King of Heaven, and carry it without fear.' According to the order of the same saints, this banner was made of white cloth, strewn with lilies. The Saviour of men was represented there seated in the midst of the clouds, on a throne placed on a rainbow, and holding the globe of the earth in His hand. At His feet, right and left, were kneeling two angels; one held a lily, which is the coat of arms of France, and to which God had blessed. As a motto, we read on the side: JHESUS, MARIA. Moreover, this banner had the shape of that of an ordinary knight; on the banner particular to this type of pennants was painted the Annunciation with an angel offering a lily to the Blessed Virgin." (*Hist. De l'Èglise*, Rohrbacher.)

෧ ✠ ഌ

---

that suddenly there were many more soldiers aiding the French as if the 'whole world' was gathered there which caused panic among their troops. This miraculous impression befuddling the English was attributed to the patron saints of the city, St. Euverte and St. Aignan. (E.A. Bucc.)

The Vow of Queen Anne of Austria

"From the abyss of my nothingness, prostrate myself at the feet of Thy August and Sacred Majesty, I am ashamed, by the sight of my sins, to appear before Thee, O my God! I recognize the just vengeance of Thy holy anger, irritated against me and against my State; and I stand, however, before you, remembering the holy words which Thou once said to the prophet, concerning a king who was a sinner, but remembered: 'I will have mercy on him, and I will forgive him, on account I see him humbled in My presence.' With this confidence, O my God! I dare to wish to erect to Thee an altar to Thy glory, under the title of Saint Michael and all the holy angels, and, under their intercession, to have there solemnly celebrated every first Tuesday of the month, the very Holy Sacrifice of the Mass, where I will be, if it pleases Thy divine goodness to suffer me there, when the important affairs of the kingdom will allow me to do so in order to obtain the peace of the Church and the State."[28]

---

28   The Vow of Queen Anne.   Anne of Austria (1601-1666) was a Spanish princess and an Austrian archduchess of the House of Habsburg.   She was married to Louis XIII and was queen of France.   She became a powerful regent of France during the minority of her son, Louis XIV, from 1643 to 1651.   The

M Olier, to impress in the heart of the queen-mother a lively confidence in Saint Michael, added to the formula of the vow, these sentiments so worthy of the piety of the most Christian kings:

"Glorious Saint Michael, prince of the militia of Heaven and general of the armies of God, I recognize thee as all powerful through Him over kingdoms and states. I submit to thee all my Court, my State, my family, and I myself renew, as much as it is in me, the piety of all the same predecessors, who have always referred to thee as their particular defender.

Therefore, out of thy love for this state, subject it all to God and to those who represent Him. Great saint, who suppressed the haughtiness of the ungodly, who banished them from heaven by making reign there a very deep peace, produce these same effects in the kingdom. May it please God, after all the troubles are subsided, to see Jesus Christ, His dear Son,

_____

vow referred to here was made during The Fronde, which was a series of civil wars that occurred in France from 1648-1653 right in the middle of the Franco-Spanish War (1635-1659). The vow was made in 1652 for the return of peace and was composed by Abbé Jean-Jacques Olier (1608-1657), who was the founder of the Séminaire de Saint-Sulpice. The monthly Masses in honour of St. Michael were charged to the monks of Mont Saint-Michel. Considering the altar was to be purposely built for the Masses, it must have been constructed at Mont Saint-Michel. (E.A. Bucc.)

reign in peace in the Church, desiring, on my part, to contribute to His reign, either through all examples of piety and religion that I can give in my person, or by the other ways on which thou will do me the grace to enlighten me. " (*Spirit of M. Olier.*)

As this vow remained undoubtedly secret, we do not know the circumstances which could accompany its accomplishment. (*Life of M. Olier.*)

෨ ❖ ෬

St. Michael and King Afonso I

In the year 1167, King Afonso I of Portugal instituted the religious and military order of Saint Michael, on the following occasion:

Afonso was in Santarem, when Albrac, Muslim king of Seville, came to besiege him with a mighty arm. Afonso, who did not expect this, had only a handful of people. In addition, he learned that the King of Leon, with whom he was not on too good an understanding, was marching on Portugal on his side, perhaps to join the infidels. In this uncertainty, King Afonso with the few people he had, marched against the

Saracens. Their multiplicity cannot shake his courage; on the contrary, convinced that God, who had exterminated by one of his angels one hundred and eighty-five thousand soldiers of the army of Sennacherib, was no less powerful to deliver him from his enemies than he had been to save Israel. He begged Him fervently to send a good angel who would march before him, and bear fear and terror into the heart of those blasphemers of His holy name, who only lived to oppress His people and profane His holy temples. His prayer was answered; he defeated the enemies completely. But at the height of the battle, realizing that the Saracens had removed the great standard of the kingdom, it dawned on the ranks to retake it, and, in this perilous action he saw he was visibly assisted by the Archangel Saint Michael. Full of gratitude, Afonso built a chapel in the Alcobaça convent, and instituted the military order of Saint Michael. (*Les Anges de Dieu aimés des hommes.*)

Additional note: This occurred during the Reconquest in which the Christian Crusaders overthrew the Muslim occupiers of the Iberian Peninsula. On March 10, 1147, King Afonso I (1101- 1111) departed for battle with only an army of 250 knights. According to tradition, due to his great devotion to St. Michael and his Guardian Angel, he saw in the sky a great winged arm bearing a sword come to aid the Christian forces during the Conquest of Santarém in 1147, which some of the captive Moors admitted they had also seen. The wing was believed to be that of St. Michael. The vision was important as it was heaven-sent evidence that Heaven was with the newly established Kingdom of Portugal, which was then only a few years old, and also sanctioned the growth of its territories.

However, contrary to the account quoted by Fr. Marin above, the King of Leon had established peace with his cousin a few years earlier in 1143 with the Treaty of Zamora and came to aid the King of Portugal. Also, the military order was not only founded to honour St. Michael, but also the King of Leon's Knights of the Order of Saint James of the Sword who came to his aid. The name of the new order founded in honour of this occasion is called the *Real Ordem Equestre e Militar de São Miguel da Ala*, (Royal Equestrian and Military Order of Saint Michael of the Wing .) The order was revived twice and continues to this day as a royal Catholic Brotherhood. Membership in the order may be bestowed upon individuals of any citizenship, religion, or gender for recognised outstanding contributions to Portuguese royal charities or for the spread of devotion to Saint Michael, traditionally venerated as Angel of Portugal and Angel of Peace. The order has been conferred on individuals of merit chosen exclusively by the Royal House of Braganza. (E.A. Bucc.)

�৪❖৪

St. Michael and St. Francis

Francis, the truly faithful servant and minister of Jesus Christ, writes Saint Bonaventure, being in prayer one morning on the mountain of Alverne, during the Lent that he used to do in honour of the glorious Saint Michael,[*] rose to God through the seraphic fervour of his desires, transforming himself, by the movements of a tender and affectionate compassion into the One who, by the excess of charity, wanted to be crucified for us, when he saw Him like a seraph, having six shining wings and all of fire, which descended towards him from the height of Heaven. This seraph came of a rapid flight into the space of air very close to the saint; and then there appeared between His wings the figure of a crucified Man, Whose hands and feet were extended and attached to a cross. His wings were arranged in such a way that He had two on the ground, that He extended two to fly, and that He covered His whole body with the other two. At the sight of such an object, Francis was extraordinarily surprised; a joy mingled with sorrows and pain spread in his soul; the presence of Jesus Christ, who showed Himself to him in the form of a seraph, in such a marvellous manncr and with so much familiarity, and with

---

[*]   'The Lent' - i.e. the forty days of Lenten-style fasting he would accomplish preceding St. Michael's feast day in honour of the Archangel.

"Saints Michael and Francis" (c. 1505–9)

Whom he saw himself regarded so favourably, gave him excess of pleasure; but the painful spectacle of His crucifixion penetrated him with compassion, and his soul was pierced by it like a sword. Above all, he wondered deeply at the weakness of sufferings that appeared in the figure of a seraph, knowing full well that it did not accord with his state of immortality, and he could not understand the purpose of this vision, when the Lord inwardly taught him, as to His friend, that He manifested Himself to him in this state to make him know that it was not through martyrdom that He so keenly desired him to endure, but through the burning of the soul, for him to be completely transformed into a perfect resemblance with Jesus crucified.

The vision, disappearing after a secret and familiar conversation, left him with a seraphic ardour in his soul, and marked his body with a figure conforming to that of the crucifix, as if flesh resembled wax softened and melted by fire, had received the printing of the characteristics of a seal. (*Life of Saint Francis of Assisi*). [29]

ॐ ❖ ॐ

29   According to St. Bonaventure, the stigmata appeared on St. Francis' hands and feet with an appearance like nails. The heads of the nails in his hands and feet were round and black, and the points were somewhat long and bent, as if they had been turned back. He also had a wound appear in his side, blood often flowed from it and stained his tunic.

St. Michael at the Time of Death

1. Preservation

M. de Quériolet having been attacked by a continuous fever five or six days before the feast day of Saint Michael, and the ardour of this fever being greater that day, he nevertheless felt so strongly drawn to attend Mass that after a long struggle with his weakness he finally got up and went to church, even while in extraordinary pain, hoping to return to bed immediately. But by a special leading of grace from God and of this glorious archangel, before returning to his room, he went into his garden and lay down on a bench where after he had rested for an hour or two, one of his servants who was very frightened ran to tell him that the floor, the beams and the girders of the attic had fallen into his room and that his bed was all crushed, which he found to be true when he returned home. He greatly thanked Saint Michael, firmly believing that the blessed Archangel, patron of our France, had preserved him from this obvious danger by his merits. So he often went to pray to him in the Chartreuse d'Auray church, which recognized him as a special patron.

Additional Note: Monsieur Quériolet, that is, Pierre Le Gouvello de Keriolet Auray (1602-1660), was from a noble family of Brittany. He was a wicked and violent child, so his parents sent him to the Jesuit college in Rennes to try and have him reformed. However, his wickedness only seemed to grow.   At the age of twenty-two he robbed his own parents and took off to live a life of sinful adventure and pillage, eventually deciding at one point to join the Turkish army, even planning on renouncing his faith and becoming a Muslim to do so. This plan was foiled when he was unable to leave Venice for Turkey. He went to Paris to live a life of debauchery and even fell into practising the occult. He eventually returned to Brittany but was still a libertine and had a lust for duelling and killed many who duelled against him. He became a solider for a period, but then inherited the family noble legacy upon his father's death. That wasn't enough, to secure more wealth he became a Protestant Huguenot. He then aspired to became a magistrate in Brittany by bribing his way in. He misused his influence to cause disputes in court so duels could be fought! An adulterer and guilty of many sacrilegious Communions, his evilness grew to the point that whenever he entered a church it was to mock the priest and the faithful. He was so great a public sinner his name was used by parents to terrify their children into good behaviour.

However by the merciful grace of God he had some good qualities left. He showed kindness to the poor and never refused them alms. He also said a Hail Mary everyday, although probably without conviction and only to fulfil a promise to his mother.   He also had a few narrow misses that no doubt made him think. Miraculously he escaped unscathed when he was fired upon at point blank range with a rifle. On another occasion, he and his horse were struck by lightning, but he was unharmed. The next near miss happened when he and two companions were set upon by robbers and it looked like they were done for. Getting on his knees he made a vow to undertake a pilgrimage to Our Lady's shrine of Notre-Dame-de-Liesse. His life was miraculously spared again, but the wretched man failed to fulfil his vow.

Then, Keriolet had a vision of hell one night which greatly troubled him – he was shown the place of torment reserved for him if he did not convert and amend his life. He went to confession, attended church and even entered a monastery, but his conversion must have been only superficial for after a week he left and relapsed into his former life, becoming worse than before.

Later in 1636 he heard of a strange occurrence happening in Loudon – all the nuns in the Ursuline convent were possessed and undergoing exorcism. Curious, he attended the exorcism sessions for four days and questioned one of the possessed nuns on the fifth day: the demon in the nun recognised him and cried out, "What! This one who has despised God for so many years! Oh, wicked one! I thought I would hold you and carry you off to hell, before you made this vow to Notre-Dame-de-Liesse that you have never fulfilled. Ungrateful and unworthy of the blessings of the Virgin!" Astonished that the possessed nun knew of his brush with death and his unfulfilled vow, he then asked what happened during the other times with the rifle fire and the lightning. The devil admitted again, "I would have carried you off if it hadn't been for the Virgin Mary and the cherubim, your Guardian Angel." He then asked why he left the monastery, no doubt to test why he couldn't stay there if he had been so graced to survive. The demon answered, confirming his conversion was superficial at best at the time without a true purpose of amendment, therefore abusing the grace given him: "God could not bear so impure a man in such a holy house. Blasphemer and atheist! Is it possible for such a man to receive mercy?"

At this, Keriolet was converted at last and in tears he publicly confessed his sins on the spot, however, falling in a heap at the feet of the priest before he could finish. He spent the whole night in tears for his sins and came to the Church the next day. The demon suddenly announced: "O people, if you knew how much I am enduring from this change, you would weep over me, yes, you would weep over the devil... He's in such a state that if he continues, he will be as high in heaven as he would have been low in hell with us!" The exorcist then demanded to know what had brought this conversion about. "It is the Virgin Mary, who is the great friend of this man. She put her arms in up to her elbows to pull him from his filth." The demon then said to Pierre, "Your measure was full, but you kept a little devotion for *her*....Oh, I'll get even with you! I'll follow you wherever you go!"

From this we can assume that the roof beams falling upon his bed was not a normal accident but an preternatural incident caused by the devil from which Pierre Keriolet was saved thanks to Our Lady and his devotion to St. Michael and the angels. He continued to live a life of austerity and became a priest. He founded a hospital for the poor in Auray. The bandit who once inspired great fear became a source of great edification and veneration. He was buried at the Sainte-Anne d'Auray basilica. (E.A. Bucc.)

2 Assistance

Saint Anselm relates that a religious of his time, very devoted to Saint Michael, was marvellously helped at the hour of death. The demon first threw at him a thousand scruples in his mind about the sins he had committed before baptism, for he had received this sacrament after the use of reason: which caused the patient to enter into several thoughts of despair. But the

great archangel, whom he invoked on this occasion, said to him: "I am with you, my son, and I will not forsake you. Answer your enemy that you know well that all your sins committed before baptism have been blotted out by virtue of this sacrament." The demon, without rebutting, gave him a second round of attack on the sins he had committed since baptism. And Saint Michael, who was present, saw the sick man was in great perplexity. "Courage," he said to him, "boldly answer that you are assured that all your sins since baptism have been forgiven you by the holy profession you have made in religion." "That is true," replied the demon, "but how many have you made since your vows?" Then Saint Michael could no longer endure the insolence of this cruel enemy of mankind, drove him out of the sickroom, saying to him: "Know that all the faults that this religious has committed since his profession have been remitted by penance, by the good deeds he has done, and by the sufferings of this last illness. Learn today that you will never have any power over those who have recourse to me and who are under my protection." As soon as the angel of God had said these words, the sick man died in peace.

Saint Arnold, bishop of Soissons,[30] experienced the protection of the Archangel in a very remarkable way. He called the people of the house on the eve of the Assumption, and ordered them to prepare everything for his funeral. How they were astonished! "The glorious Archangel Saint Michael brought me this good news yesterday," he told them, "and he promised me that he would come at the head of the blessed spirits to carry my soul into Heaven. In fact, having asked for and received the last sacraments, lying on the ground on sackcloth

---

30   St. Arnoul, or Arnold (c. 1040- 1187) was a French nobleman and had a distinguished career as a solider under King Robert and King Henry I of France. He gave up his noble life and became a monk at the Benedictine monastery of St. Medard at Soissons, eventually electing to lead a very austere life of prayer of penance as hermit by a shutting himself up in a narrow cell, a life which lasted for three and a half years until he was chosen to be abbot of the monastery, a dignity which he tried to avoid by fleeing but a wolf miraculously forced him to return.   He then was elected bishop of Soissons, another dignity he tried to avoid.   Eventually he retired from public life and founded the Abbey of St. Peter in Oudenberg. While abbot of his monastery, he brewed beer and encouraged the local peasants to drink it instead of water that was unsafe at the time. It is said many of the inhabitants around the monastery were saved during a plague as the water was infected, but the beer was safe to drink due to the brewing process. He is therefore the patron saint of brewers.

and on ashes, he returned his soul to God, strengthened and visited by Saint Michael, by his good angel and by the blessed spirits who accompanied him to Heaven.

ഔ❖ഔ

The Celestial Procession Attending the Vatican Council - December 8, 1869

"On December 8, during my thanksgiving, Our Lord, undoubtedly to compensate me for why He had not healed me, was kind enough to make me enjoy a magnificent spectacle, by letting me see the celestial procession that was going to the Council. I doubt that the procession in Rome, beautiful as it was, can be compared to the one I saw.

The Archangel Saint Michael led the way: he carried a standard on which was written in Latin these words,"Who is like unto God?" After him, Our Lord and the Blessed Virgin, standing on a sort of cloud formed by a multitude of angels. Our Lord with one of His arms seemed to support the Blessed Virgin, who held in her hand a lily of dazzling whiteness. In front of her walked the angel Gabriel who also carried a standard on which read, always in Latin, "Queen conceived without sin! ..." After them came Saint Peter carrying the keys. He was also preceded by

147

an angel on whose banner was written: "Thou art Peter, and upon this rock I will build My Church, and the gates of Hell shall not prevail against it." After Saint Peter came Saint John the Evangelist, also preceded by an angel carrying a standard on which read: "The Word was made flesh and dwelt amongst us." All the other apostles came next, and they were followed by all the Holy Popes who have existed since the founding of the Church - Myriads of angels surrounded and followed this imposing procession.

At the moment when it disappeared before my eyes, I heard all the bells of Rome ringing as if in the distance, and this peal gave me a moment of joy and distraction."

(*From the letters of Mlle. Guillemaut of pious memory.*)

It is always with the same reservations[*] made previously in the other numbers of this correspondence, that we quote the writings of this privileged soul.

V. DREVON, S.J.

---

[*]   'Reservations' – i.e. the customary reservations applying in that while quoting this letter, the author submits to the Church regarding any future decision regarding Mlle. Guillemaut's writings as she was not yet an officially approved mystic. This means he intended no disobedience at the time if in the future the Church ruled against her. So far to date, there appears to be no negative ruling on Mlle. Guillemaut or her writings.

Additional Note: When quoting this story Fr. Marin must have assumed his readers would know about Mlle. Léonie Guillemaut (1812- 1872) and her mystical experiences, which may not be the case today.   Therefore I am adding a short biography here into the original text.

Mlle. Louise-Charlotte-Pauline-Léonie Guillemaut was a French Catholic author who wrote numerous devotional books in the 19th century, and it appears she was a special victim soul. Her father came from a good family in Louhans, while on her mother's side she descended from the ancient noble line of the Branges. Her mother first taught her the principles of the faith and later she went for her schooling to the nuns of Saint-Maur. Already at the age of four she delighted in prayer, giving alms to the poor from the allowance her parents gave her, attending Mass, and would spend long hours in adoration before the Blessed Sacrament, thereby by the age of twelve she had already gained a reputation for virtue and piety.

As her virtues continued to grow, she was ordered by her spiritual director to write down all that occurred in her soul and all the favours granted to her by God. Through her writings it is evident her virtues only increased as her life of suffering increased – she lost her father at a young age, other family misfortunes also followed, her health declined sharply with various ailments and sufferings, her childhood friends left her, all this in addition to the various spiritual sufferings and dark nights of the soul she suffered, all for the salvation of souls and in preparation for the next favours God would grant her. She became a member of the Franciscan Third Order and made a vow of perpetual virginity since due to her ill health she was unable to join a religious order, however, God favoured her with visions. She was always obedient to her spiritual director and the Church, and wrote down all her experiences, many were also recorded in letters, as in the example we see above regarding the vision of the Heavenly procession she saw during the First Vatican Council.   It is believed her prayer and meditation books

149

were inspired by the Heavenly favours she received. She died in Louhans on Good Friday, March 29, 1872.

Information from the obituary of Léonie Guillemaut written by Mgr. Guillaume-Marie- Frédéric Bouange (1814-1884), Vicar General of Autun and then Bishop of Langres, quoted on pp. 30-34 in 'Le Messager du Coeur de Jésus', Tome XXI, Janiever-Juin, 1872. Other source, 'Vie de Mgr Bouange, (Guillaume-Marie-Frédéric), évêque de Langres'. By Abbé Guillaume Delmas, (1885).

Mgr. Bouange was one of her spiritual directors and received many communications from her. He hoped that one day her life would become well-known and her letters made available, but she seems to have fallen into obscurity. A few of her devotional prayer books are still available in French reprint editions. (E.A. Bucc.)

ဆာ❖ca

The Angel of Judgement Day

"'As soon as the signal has been given by the voice of the archangel and the sound of the trumpet of God,' says Saint Paul, 'the Lord himself will come down from heaven, and those who are dead in Jesus Christ will be resurrected first.'

'The Archangel Saint Michael', says Saint

Thomas, 'at the command of Christ, will sound the trumpet': this trumpet will first sound these words, 'Prepare yourselves, the Judge is here!'. These are the expressions of Saint John Chrysostom.

'And the Son of Man', saith the Saviour, 'will send out His angels with a trumpet and a great voice.'

Once again the archangel will sound, and the angels will repeat with a loud voice and with solemnity: 'Dead, arise!' Then God will revive the ashes of every one; the angels will gather the elect from the four winds and carry them to the valley of Jehoshaphat, where, according to Joel, the judgement will take place. 'I will gather all the nations,' he said, 'and bring them into the valley of Jehoshaphat, and I will plead with them.'.

"When men, having already undergone the judgement of their eternity, will see themselves in the presence of all the nations, on the point of either being glorified or confounded, there will be time for the cry of conscience, so long stifled.

At this time the Cross will appear carried by the angels, to the testimony of the Holy Fathers, and probably by Saint Michael, called the Standard Bearer. A mixed cry of astonishment and desolation will arise from all the nations of the earth.

The Son of Man will be seen coming in the clouds of heaven.

"St. Michael and the Dragon" (1860)

"The Ancient of Days having sat face to face with the angels and the hoary generations of all the ages, He will justify His wisdom, His justice and His mercy: the righteous will be manifested with all the good they have done in secret: the wicked, conquered by their crimes, will bear their public shame on their foreheads.

And the sentence will be pronounced! ....

"And I saw an angel coming down from heaven, having the key of the bottomless pit, and a great chain in his hand. And he laid hold on the dragon the old serpent, which is the devil and Satan and bound him ... And he cast him into the bottomless pit, and shut him up, and set a seal upon him...."

Saint Michael has thus consummated the victory.

(Delmas, *S. Michel et les saints Anges*.)

In her revelations, the Sister of the Nativity relates, as follows, the terrible scene of Last Judgement:

'When the Antichrist, triumphing over his victories in the quarrel which he will declare to the Church, will arm himself to crush and abolish it as he will believe, God will send the great archangel Saint Michael to the head of his Church with troops of angels who will surround him .... God made known to me the superbly evil intentions of Satan and his satellites. They will rise to heaven with great joy and great triumph, purposely going to quarrel with the Eternal Being, to raise their throne above His and to destroy Him, if they could, aspiring to a glory like that of Lucifer. It is in this moment that God will send the great Archangel Saint Michael, clothed with strength and righteousness from above, who will come from heaven to meet them with a threatening air and who will bring terror among the infernal spirits.

'Our Lord will make His voice heard through the breath of the Archangel Saint Michael and will say: 'Go, accursed, descend to the depths of the abysses of Hell.' Instantly, the earth will open up and present a frightful chasm of fire and flame into which this unwavering cohort will fall pell-mell ... and, all will go to the bottom of the abyss forever.'"

Additional Note: Sr. Jeanne de Le Royer of the Nativity (1731-1798) was born into a poor family in the little village of Beaulot not far from Fougères in Brittany, France. From an early age she discerned a vocation to enter the religious life, and making a vow of chastity, she overcame all the temptations opposed to her vocation and her vow. She was devoted to her guardian angel, Our Lady, and also to the Blessed Sacrament. At the age of fifteen or sixteen she lost her father, she then planned to live with her mother in order to support her, but her mother died soon as well, and Jeanne, who was then left destitute had no other desire than to obtain admission into some convent as a servant, the better to keep her vow of chastity. She wished to enter the convent of the Urbanists at Fougères, a Poor Clare convent. It appears she was met with some opposition to entering due to her inability to pay the required dowry, but at last she was admitted as a charitable entrant. Upon taking the vows she assumed the name of Sister Nativité, or Sister of the Nativity as she has become known in English.

Sister of the Nativity lived a life of penance and mortification with vigils, fasting, haircloth and self-flagellation forming a part of her spiritual regimen. She sometimes laid thistles and nettles in her bed, one day she was surprised in the act of sipping gall mixed with other things equally disgusting as an act of mortification. She once suffered a tumour on the knee which continued to grow after an operation, but it was miraculously cured after a novena was offered for her by the sisters of the convent. While she was cured this one time, she suffered other health complaints throughout her life.

As her virtues increased, so did other spiritual gifts, for she was given the gift of reading of hearts, she foretold to several people what would happen to them, and she was granted many visions, including those of the future, and even of the Last Judgement as seen above. Her visions were written down by her spiritual director, Abbé Genet, who she told not to release them until the 'indicated time' had come. Apparently, she revealed to him when her visions should be released, which was some time after her death. She died on the Assumption of 1798, with the crucifix before her, the vows of her profession on her breast, and holy water at her side, with which according to her desire, she was repeatedly sprinkled. She was buried in the cemetery of Languelet.

Abbé Genet published the first edition of her visions in 1817 under the title, "*Vie et révélations de la Soeur Nativité, religieuse converse au couvent des Urbanistes de Fougères*" and it went through several reprints. While there has been no official pronouncement of her visions, there does not appear to be any official condemnation of them either to date. (E.A. Bucc.)

HYMN TO ST. MICHAEL

200 days indulgence if said once a day.

For the daily recitation for a month, a plenary indulgence.

Te splendor et virtus Patris,
Te vita, Jesu, cordium,
Ab ore qui pendent tuo,
Laudamus inter Angelos.
 Tibi mille densa millium
Ducum corona militat:
Scul explicat victor crucem
Michael salutis signifer.
 Draconis hic dirum caput
In ima pellit tartara,
Ducemque cum rebellibus
Coelesti ab arce fulminat.
Contra ducem superbiae
Sequamur hunc nos Principem,
Ut detur ex Agni throno
Nobis corona gloriae.
Patri, simulque Filio,
Tibique sancte Spiritus,
Sicut fuit, sit jugiter,
Saeclum per omne gloria. Amen.

Ant. Princeps gloriosissime, Michael Archangele, esto memor nostri: hic et ubique semper precare pro nobis Filium Dei.

V. In conspectu angelorum psallam tibi, Deus meus.

R. Adorabo ad templum sanctum tuum, et confitebor nomini tuo.

Oremus.

Deus, qui miro ordine angelorum ministeria hominumque dispensas: concede propitius, ut, a quibus tibi ministrantibus in coelo semper assistitur, ab his in terra vita nostra muniatur. Per Dominum nostrum Jesus Christum Filium tuum, qui Tecum vivit et regnat in unitate Spiritus Sancti, Deus, per omnia saecula saeculorum. Amen.

TRANSLATION

O Jesu, life-spring of the soul,
The Father's power, and glory bright!
Thee with the angels we extol;
From Thee they draw their life and light.
Thy thousand thousand hosts are spread
Embattled o'er the azure sky;
But Michael bears Thy standard dread,
And lifts the mighty Cross on high.
He in that sign the rebel powers
Did with their dragon prince expel;
And hurl'd them from
the heaven's high towers
Down like a thunderbolt to hell.
Grant us with Michael still, O Lord,
Against the Prince of Pride to fight;
So may a crown be our reward,
Before the Lamb's pure throne of light.
To God the Father glory be,
And to his sole-begotten SonThe same,
O Holy Ghost, to Thee
While everlasting ages run. Amen.

Ant. Most glorious Prince, Michael the
Archangel, be thou mindful of us; here, and in all
places, pray for us to the Son of God most high.

V. I wilt sing praises to Thee, my God,
before the Angels.
R. I will adore Thee in Thy holy temple,
and praise Thy Name.

Let us pray.

O God, who in the dispensation of Thy providence dost admirably dispose the ministry of angels and of men; mercifully grant that the Holy Angels, who ever minister before Thy throne in heaven, may be the protectors also of our life on earth. Through Jesus Christ our Lord Thy Son, who liveth and reigneth with Thee in the unity of the Holy Ghost, one God, world without end. Amen.[31]

ഇ❖ദ

---

31   This hymn to St. Michael from the Roman Breviary is known as the 'Te splendor et virtus Patris' and is by Pope Urban VII.   He drew upon the hymn *Tibi, Christe, splendor Patris* for inspiration, which is attributed to St. Rabanus Maurus (776-856 AD), a Frankish Benedictine monk, theologian, poet, encyclopedist and military writer who became archbishop of Mainz.   Regarding the Indulgences mentioned: the hymn to St. Michael 'Te splendor et virtus Patris' is included in the Raccolta collection of prayers with indulgences, and its authorized translations. In 1817 Pope Pius VII granted an indulgence of 200 days once a day for saying the hymn, including the antiphon and closing prayer, with a contrite heart and devotion, in honour of St. Michael the Archangel in order to obtain his patronage and protection against the assaults of the enemy of man.   He also granted a plenary indulgence for saying the hymn every day consecutively for a month, together with the usual conditions of Confession and Communion, and praying for the intentions of the pope.

The Chaplet of Saint Michael

I. ~ Promises of the Holy Archangel.

Saint Michael appeared to the most great servant of God, Antónia de Astónaco, and said that he wished to be honoured by nine salutations corresponding to the nine choirs of angels, and that would consist of an Our Father and three Hail Marys in honour of each of the nine choirs.

He promised in return to whoever would venerate him in this way, that before Holy Communion, he obtained the grace he would assign an angel from each of the nine choirs to accompany them as they approached the Holy Table. Moreover, to those who would recite these nine salutations every day, he promised his continual assistance during their life, as well as of all the holy angels, and he added that after death he would obtain the deliverance of their soul and those of their relations from the penalties of Purgatory. This is what is reported in the life of the saint, in book II, chap. LXXIV.

(Note: The Chaplet or 'Crown' of St. Michael is said on a set of special chaplet beads similar to a rosary, but instead of five decades, there are nine sections, each with one bead for the Our Father followed by three beads for the Hail Marys to be said after the Nine Salutations. The chaplet concludes with four other beads from which hangs the medal of St. Michael. - E.A. Bucc)

"The Nine Choirs of Celestial Spirits" (1679)

II. ~Indulgences granted by Pius IX

-1st: Indulgence of 7 years and 7 quarantaines (i.e. 7 years and 280 days) each time the chaplet is said. -2nd: 100 days each day when you carry it or when you kiss the medal; - 3rd Plenary indulgence to those who pray it once a month, the day they choose, truly contrite and having confessed, praying for the intentions of their Holiness.   Also, plenary indulgence with the same conditions and if said on these feast days of the Apparition of St Michael the Archangel (May 8); the feast of the Archangels Michael, Gabriel and Raphael (September 29); and on the day of the Holy Guardian Angels (October 2).

III. ~ Manner in Serving – **HOW TO PRAY THE CHAPLET**

Each person is to make a sincere act of contrition, kneel before an image of the holy Archangel and piously recite the following salutations.

After making the sign of the cross, on the medal the beginning verse is said, the response, and then the Glory Be.

V: O God, come to my assistance.
R. O Lord, make haste to help me.
Glory Be....

First Salutation:

By the intercession of St. Michael and the celestial Choir of Seraphim may the Lord make us worthy to burn with the fire of perfect charity. Amen. (*Next Say the Our Father and Three Hail Marys to the First Choir of Angels.*)

Second Salutation:

By the intercession of St. Michael and the celestial Choir of Cherubim may the Lord grant us the grace to leave the ways of sin and run in the paths of Christian perfection. Amen. (*Say the Our Father and Three Hail Marys to the Second Choir of Angels.*)

Third Salutation:

By the intercession of St. Michael and the celestial Choir of Thrones may the Lord infuse into our hearts a true and sincere spirit of humility. Amen. (*Say the Our Father and Three Hail Marys to the Third Choir of Angels.*)

Fourth Salutation:

By the intercession of St. Michael and the celestial Choir of Dominions may the Lord give us grace to govern our senses and overcome any unruly passions. *(Say the Our Father and Three Hail Marys to the Fourth Choir of Angels.)*

Fifth Salutation:

By the intercession of St. Michael and the celestial Choir of Powers may the Lord protect our souls against the snares and temptations of the devil. Amen. (*Say the Our Father and three Hail Marys to the Fifth Choir of Angels.*)

Sixth Salutation:

By the intercession of St. Michael and the celestial Choir of Virtues may the Lord preserve us from evil and falling into temptation. Amen. (*Say the Our Father and three Hail Marys to the Sixth Choir of Angels.*)

Seventh Salutation:

By the intercession of St. Michael and the celestial Choir of Principalities may God fill our souls with a true spirit of obedience. Amen. (Say the Our Father and three Hail Marys to the Seventh Choir of Angels.)

Eighth Salutation:

By the intercession of St. Michael and the celestial Choir of Archangels may the Lord give us perseverance in faith and in all good works in order that we may attain the glory of Heaven. Amen. (Say the Our Father and three Hail Marys to the Eighth Choir of Angels.)

By the intercession of St. Michael and the celestial Choir of Angels may the Lord grant us to be protected by them in this mortal life and conducted in the life to come to Heaven. Amen. (Say the Our Father and three Hail Marys to the Ninth Choir of Angels.)

On the four beads next to the medal, say an Our Father, each in honour of St. Michael, St. Gabriel, St. Raphael and your Guardian Angel. Then conclude with the following prayers.

O glorious prince St. Michael, chief and commander of the heavenly hosts, guardian of souls, vanquisher of rebel spirits, servant in the house of the Divine King and our admirable conductor, you who shine with excellence and superhuman virtue deliver us from all evil, who turn to you with confidence and enable us by your gracious protection to serve God more and more faithfully every day.

V. Pray for us, O glorious St. Michael, Prince of the Church of Jesus Christ,

R. That we may be made worthy of His promises.

Concluding Prayer:

Almighty and Everlasting God, Who, by a prodigy of goodness and a merciful desire for the salvation of all men, has appointed the most glorious Archangel St. Michael Prince of Your Church, make us worthy, we ask You, to be delivered from all our enemies, that none of them may harass us at the hour of death, but that we may be conducted by him into Your Presence. This we ask through the merits of Jesus Christ Our Lord. Amen.

ഇ ❖ ൦

The History of the Chaplet[32]

The origin of the chaplet is shrouded in history and also some controversy. The general information given is that St. Michael allegedly appeared to a Portuguese Carmelite Nun named Antónia d'Astónaco, also called Antoniá de Astronac, to whom he requested that the salutations be composed in addition to revealing a series of promises that would be granted. While the vision of the Archangel to Antónia is said to have happened c. 1750 -1751, there is evidence the chaplet attributed to Sr. Antónia existed long before this time as 1655 is the earliest recorded date associated with this chaplet. The chaplet was then promoted by a another sister named Maria Angela Colomba Leonardi at the Vetralla

---

32   As this information is too long for a footnote it has been
     placed here as a new addition to Fr. de Boylesve's original
     text. E.A. Bucc.

Convent in the Diocese of Viterbo, Italy, who died in 1751. This also explains why Sr. Antónia is said to have lived at the Vetralla Convent in Viterbo, which is not true. The history of these two sisters have been confused into one event.

To begin untangling the threads, we shall start with Sr. Antónia to whom the chaplet is first attributed to. Nearly all sources say she was a Venerable, or a Servant of God, but that is not a clear indication a canonisation process was opened in her case as pious mystics were also described as 'Venerable' and 'Servants of God' in older texts.

According to the website by Enzo Panepinto, the Vatican Secret Archives office has been contacted regarding Sr. Antónia and sent the following reply:

"(....) there was no reference to the Servant of God of your interest : I invite you to contact the Congregation for the Causes of Saints directly with the hope of a much more fruitful outcome ".

The Congregation was therefore contacted and this was the result:

" ... I inform you that among the documentation preserved in the Archives of this Dicastery, there is no reference to the aforementioned person ...".

Therefore, Sr. Antónia may simply have been a holy mystic and only received the titles Servant of God and Venerable as marks of respect, not as an indication of having a process of canonisation open.

Panepinto then presents information sent by the Carmelites of Vetralla:

"Many people ask us the same questions, but we must all give the same answer: first of all we are not sure that Antonia d'Astonaco was a Carmelite nun. We know what it is possible to obtain from

common sources about her, but nothing more. Devotion to St. Michael the Archangel has existed for centuries in our monastery, but this is mainly due to one of our nuns who in the past obtained from the Pope (through a family member who worked at the Holy See) the indulgence for the recitation of the angelic crown."

In all, Sr. Antónia never lived there and it was another nun who spread devotion to the chaplet at the convent who succeeded in having its promises approved.[33]

In fact, if we delve further back in history, Sr. Antónia's 'angelic crown' devotion to the angels was not the first. The earliest version of an 'Angelic Chaplet' dates from the 13th century. According to one tradition the Benedictine mystic St. Mechtilde of Hachborn (1240-1299) fervently prayed for a way to properly honour the angels. Our Lord appeared and said to honour them she should say nine Paters, i.e. Our Fathers. However, this does not appear to be a well known devotion of St. Mechtilde, so this tradition as having originated from her revelations is questionable. Her devotions had become so popular that unscrupulous souls began spreading made-up devotions in her name. Nevertheless, it is possible this early 'Angelic Chaplet' was either confused with or inspired by another authentic revelation given to St. Mechtilde regarding a holy way to prepare for a feast day of Our Lord, Our Lady or the Angels by saying beforehand a novena of nine Ave Marias. Therefore, this nine day novena could have been the

---

33   Source of the information: Enzo Panepinto, 'Doni Dal Cielo', 2012-2016. Site address:
http://donidalcielo.blogspot.com/2016/05/la-coroncina-angelica.html

original inspiration of the 'Angelic Chaplet'. Also, there is the devotion of the Three Aves in honour of Our Lady's purity that was attributed to St. Mechtilde as well, (although first practised by St Anthony of Padua), which could also have been tripled and turned into a Nine Aves novena.

After this, we see a Nine Ave 'Angelic Crown' was spread in Italy according to evidence in a book of sermons by Fr. Serafino Razzi dated 1590 entitled: "Sermoni predicabili dalla prima domenica dell'Avvento, fino all'ottava di Pasqua di resurrezione". He also included it in a five volume work called 'Della Corona Angelica', (Lucca 1599). Fr. Razzi's rendition is a devotion to Our Lady, namely, a 'greeting' to her composed with an 'Angelic Crown' of nine Ave Marias, apparently with one Ave for each of the nine choirs of Angels.[34] Therefore, either the Nine Aves Novena, plus the Three Aves Devotion attributed to St. Mechtilde grew to what we recognise today.

The earliest mention of the St. Michael's angelic Crown with its associated promises as attributed to Sr. Antónia is dated 1655 and found in a work by the Dominican priests Frs. Hyacinthe Serrao and Vincenzo Cestari. Their text was reprinted in 1664, then in 1688 with the title "Directory and handbook very useful for the exercise of the holy mission". Panepinto notes this is the earliest passage that mentions "Book II Chapter 74" of Sr. Antónia's lost biography. He quotes the passage from the 1688 edition printed in Trani:

"Crown of the Angels, revealed by
the Most Glorious Prince St. Michael to

---

34   Ibid.

the Blessed Antonia of Astonaco, as read in her life in chap. 74 inserted in this Directory, at the request of the physicist Vincenzo Cestari di Montesano, currently living in the Sagra Certosa di S. Lorenzo della Padula.

This Crown has nine parts, corresponding to the nine Choirs of Angels, each part a Pater Noster and three Ave Maria; because the Angelic army is divided into three Hierarchies, in the end there is said four Pater Nosters.

The first in honour of S. Michele. The second in honour of St. Gabriel, the third in honour of St. Raphael, & the fourth in honour of the Angel of the Pietà.

Whoever recites the aforementioned Crown before Communion will be accompanied by nine Angels from each Angelic Choir to Communion and by the most priestly Blood of the sweet Christ, the face of the soul will be washed there, to worthily communicate. Whoever recites the said Crown every day will be aided in death and consoled by the same number of Angels, who with their effective protection will obtain liberation from the pains of Hell; and of Purgatory. In addition, if anyone recites it every day, all his relatives, if they are in Purgatory, will be visited nine times a day by the Angels, and consoled. Printed in Trani by Lorenzo Valerii 1655. with license from Superiori; and again reprinted in Trani in 1664".[35]

---

35   Ibid.

Therefore, there is evidence the Chaplet with its associated promises was first spread among the Dominicans.

The Chaplet was then promoted in 1668 by Sr. Maria Felice Spinelli (1621-1682), Foundress and First Abbess of the Capuchin Convent of Santa Maria degli Angeli on the Isola delle Grazie in Venice, under Pope Paul V. In the biography of Sr. Spinelli written by Tommaso Baldassini (Venice 1752), it is said she was very devoted to the angels, and, seeing the spiritual fruit of this chaplet, began to ardently promote it among the sisters.

We know Sr. Antónia's chaplet was also promoted among Dominican friars in Naples in the mid 1600s in a manuscript dated 1672 in the General Archives of the Order of Preachers, (MS cdn 109), again showing evidence it first appeared with the Dominican order. The same manuscript also tell us controversy arose as the friars were brought before the Inquisition because of it. The Archbishop of Naples, Cardinal Caracciolo, had stumbled across a leaflet promoting the Chaplet and referred the matter to the Holy Office, which then gave a negative decision regarding the devotion December 7, 1675. The Cardinal condemned it accordingly complete with " (...) *inquisitorial penalties all those who recite such devotion in private or in public, to anyone who publishes the said sheet or promotes the invented devotion.*"[36]

Despite this condemnation the devotion made its way to the Carmelite Covent at Vetralla in Viterbo. How it got there is still a mystery, but it was still devoutly recited by the pious soul, Sr. Maria Angela Colomba Leonardi, who encouraged the sisters to say

---

36   Ibid.

it and thereby the devotion was preserved. Born in Lucca in 1685, Sr. Maria Angela was very young when she became a Carmelite nun and made her religious profession in 1701. As a victim soul she remained completely paralysed for thirty-four years except for her hands until her death. Her confessor, St. Paul of the Cross (1694-1775), greatly admired her heroic life of sacrificial suffering. She died in 1751, hence the date of the 'vision' of St. Michael to Sr. Antónia Antonaco, which happened many years earlier, was confused with the death of Sr. Maria Angela.

As mentioned, the sisters of the convent of Vetralla kept the devotion alive. In fact, it is said Sr. Maria Angela prayed that one day after one hundred have passed years the Chaplet would be approved for the aid of Holy Mother Church as it would need the Archangel's assistance in then. Perhaps she had received some revelation that the devotion had indeed been given in a vision by the Archangel and it would be needed when the attacks against the Church would grow.

The task of bringing this devotion to the attention of the Holy See fell to another sister named Ven. Sr. Maria Felice Spinelli (1789-1850), Foundress of the Institute of the Augustinian Sisters Servants of Jesus and Mary in Frosinone. She is not to be confused with the Sister of the Capuchin convent in the previous century, yet, the remarkable occurrence of having the same name as the Capuchin sister who spread the devotion long before the Carmelite Sr. Maria Angela in Ventralla practised it seems to be a sign of Heavenly Providence. Ven. Sr. Spinelli asked her brother for assistance in having the Chaplet approved as he was employed in the Superior Government. He appealed to Mon. Dominic Gigli, who was Substitute of the Sacred Congregation of Rites. The Holy See reserved the right to approve the devotion and the indulgences requested, which occurred in 1851. Approval was also granted for the indulgences to be applicable to the souls in Purgatory. Then September 3, 1868, Pius IX granted the plenary indulgence under the usual conditions to those who visit the Carmelite church of Vetralla on the feast of St. Michael the Archangel (Sept 29) or on one of the days immediately preceding or following; this indulgence is also applicable to the dead. Hence, this forever sealed the connection of the Chaplet with the convent of Vetralla and caused the confusion with the location of Sr. Antónia Antonaco.

Unfortunately, there still remains very little to no information at all regarding Sr. Antónia Antonaco to whom the devotion is first attributed. She is not an official Servant of God, nor a Venerable or Blessed with a canonisation process. She is described as a Portuguese nun, that the vision happened in Portugal, and that she at least lived sometime in the early to mid 17th century according to the earliest sources and not the 18th. It is also possible she may have been a Dominican and not a Carmelite as we have seen the earliest texts give evidence the devotion first prevailed with the Dominicans. So, she was accidentally connected with the Carmelites of Vetralla. However, as there is no evidence of a nun with this name having ever existed except through texts referring to this devotion, it has been suggested 'Antiona de Antonaco' could be a pseudonym of the nun who had the vision as she may have desired to remain hidden as an act humility. Therefore, we may never know anything more about her as she and her biography, of which no extant copy remains, is lost to history. It is thanks to the various religious who discovered the devotion through the centuries that mention of her and the 'Angelic Crown' continued.

Regarding the current form of the promises: the Church approved the promise that the relatives of the devout practitioners could be released from Purgatory, when in the earliest texts the Angel only promised their relatives would be visited and consoled by the angels nine times a day, we note this is a blessed revision of the original. However, the promise as written in c. 1655 that the devout practitioner would 'be released from the pains of Hell' was removed as no one can be released from Hell once condemned there! This odd line, possibly the work of a careless scribe, may have been the reason why the devotion was condemned in the 1600s by the Inquisition. Perhaps what was meant was the soul would receive all the necessary graces to secure salvation and escape damnation, however, the Church may have removed this promise from the list altogether to avoid causing confusion. (E.A. Bucc.)

છ❖ભ

"St. Michael Presenting His Arms To The Virgin Mary"

Litany of St. Michael

Lord, have mercy on us.
  Christ, have mercy on us.
Lord, have mercy on us.

Christ, hear us.
  Christ, graciously hear us.

God, the Father of Heaven,
        have mercy on us.
God, the Son, Redeemer of the world,
        have mercy on us.
God, the Holy Ghost,
        have mercy on us.

Holy Trinity, one God, *have mercy on us.*

Holy Mary, Queen of Angels, *pray for us.*

St. Michael, *pray for us.*
St. Michael, filled with the wisdom of God,
        pray for us.
St. Michael, perfect adorer of the Incarnate
  Word, *pray for us.*
St. Michael, crowned with honour and glory,
        pray for us.
St. Michael, most powerful Prince of the
  armies of the Lord, *pray for us.*

St. Michael, standard-bearer of the Most Holy
  Trinity, *pray for us.*
St. Michael, victor over Satan, *pray for us.*
St. Michael, guardian of Paradise, *pray for us.*
St. Michael, guide and comforter of the people of
  Israel, *pray for us.*
St. Michael, splendour and fortress of the Church
  Militant, *pray for us.*
St. Michael, honour and joy of the Church
  Triumphant, *pray for us.*
St. Michael, light of angels, *pray for us.*
St. Michael, bulwark of orthodox believers,
      pray for us.
St. Michael, strength of those who fight under
  the standard of the Cross, *pray for us.*
St. Michael, light and confidence of souls at the
  hour of death, *pray for us.*
St. Michael, our most sure aid, *pray for us.*
St. Michael, our help in all adversities,
      pray for us.
St. Michael, herald of the everlasting sentence,
      pray for us
St. Michael, consoler of souls detained in the
  flames of Purgatory, *pray for us.*
St. Michael, whom the Lord hath charged to
  receive souls after death, *pray for us.*
St Michael, our prince, *pray for us.*
St Michael, our advocate, *pray for us.*

Lamb of God, who takes away the sins
  of the world, *spare us, O Lord.*

Lamb of God, who takes away the sins
  of the world, *graciously hear us, O Lord.*

Lamb of God, who takes away the sins
  of the world, *have mercy on us.*

Christ, hear us.
  Christ, graciously hear us.

V. Pray for us, O glorious St Michael, Prince
   of the Church of Jesus Christ,

R. That we may be made worthy of His
promises.

Let us pray. Sanctify us, we beseech Thee,
O Lord Jesus, with Thy holy blessing, and grant
us, by the intercession of St Michael, that
wisdom which teaches us to lay up treasures in
Heaven by exchanging the goods of this world for
those of eternity, Thou Who livest and reignest,
world without end. Amen.

ഇ ❖ ര

Prayer Upon Choosing St. Michael as a Special Protector

An Act of Consecration to St. Michael

O Great prince of Heaven, most faithful guardian of the Church, St. Michael the Archangel, I (say your name here), although most unworthy to appear before you, but nonetheless trusting in thy special goodness, touched by the excellence of thine admirable prayers and the multitude of thy benefits, I present myself before thee accompanied by my guardian angel and in the presence of all the angels of Heaven to witness my devotion to thee; today I choose thee for my special protector and particular advocate, and I firmly propose to honour thee always and to make thee honoured with all my power. Assist me throughout my life so I will never offend the most pure eyes of God, either in work, or word, or thought. Defend me against all the temptations of the demon, especially regarding faith and purity, and at the hour of death, instil peace to my soul and introduce it to the eternal homeland. Amen.

৪০ ❖ ୦୫

The Archconfraternity of the Archangel St. Michael Established at the Ancient Abbey of Mont Saint-Michel (Manche) **

I- The Aim of the Archconfraternity

This Archconfraternity, approved by the Bishop of Coutances et d'Avranches, the 16th of October 1867, and confirmed by the Briefs of the Most Holy Father Pope Pius IX, on the date of the 12th of February 1869 and the 12th of May 1874, which he enriched with several indulgences, the purpose of which was to honour the most holy angels and in particular the Archangel Saint Michael, and to obtain by their intercession:

** NOTICE: this Archconfraternity is defunct and no longer in existence. However, as the following information is in Fr. Marin de Boylesve´s original book, it is included here. We can hope that the Archconfraternity will one day be re-established. Eventhough the Archconfraternity is not in existence it its old form, the faithful may still avail of graces associated with the Confraternity of the St. Michael Scapular, and also the new association of the Devotional Knights of St. Michael the Archangel. See the Appendix for more information on the Scapular and the Knights. Perhaps we can also hope that members of the new Confraternity and Devotional Knights may also avail of the graces of the old Archconfraternity of Mont Saint-Michel if practised in faith?

1. A Special protection from Heaven for the Church, the Sovereign Pontiff and for France;
2. The Preservation against a sudden and unprovided death, and above all the grave of a happy death;
3. The deliverance of souls from Purgatory.

II- Motives of the Association

1st - The importance of various purposes indicated above;

2nd- The intention of our Holy Father who has formally expressed, in the aforementioned Briefs, the desire to see this Archconfraternity take, day by day, greater increases, and with this intention, enriches it with several plenary and partial indulgences, and in particular an indulgence for any work of piety or charity made by its associates;

3rd – The numerous and powerful help that the Archconfraternity assures, at the hour of death, to all the people who are part of it, by means of the prayers which are made, each day, in the said Archconfraternity, to obtain for them the necessary graces in that supreme moment;

4th - The prayers and good works accomplished by the members of the Archconfraternity in favour of the souls in Purgatory,

5th- The Masses said at the seat of the Association, the Tuesday of each week, the day consecrated to the holy angels, for the aims of the Archconfraternity.

III – Required Conditions

The only condition to be admitted as a member of the associates is an inscription of the name of the person in the general register of Mont Saint-Michel. The printed form of admission, which is usually given, is not necessary. A person becomes a member from the moment that his, or her, name has been enrolled by the Director, or by a Zelator or Zelatrice, who has received this title from the Director, and can forthwith gain the Plenary Indulgence attached to reception, on any day at will. They can also inscribe the names of the deceased so that they may benefit by the petitions of the Archconfraternity.

IV – Indulgences Accorded to the Associates

The formality of the one time inscription fulfils, and one may gain a plenary indulgence:

- On the day of reception.
- The principal Feasts of the Archconfraternity.
- Christmas Day.

- Assumption of the Blessed Virgin.

- Feast of St. Michael.

- SS. Peter and Paul.

- At the hour of death, with the usual conditions of confession and communion, or, when these conditions cannot be fulfilled, by invoking with the lips, or at least from the heart, the Holy Name of Jesus

An Indulgence of seven years and seven times forty days may be gained on the Feasts of the Archconfraternity, as also other partial Indulgences granted by the Holy See, and especially an Indulgence of sixty days every time that any work of piety or charity shall have been performed. All these Indulgences are applicable to the souls in Purgatory.

V - Feasts of the Archconfraternity.

1. The Dedication of St. Michael, September 29

2. The Holy Angel Guardians, October 2.

3. The Apparition of St. Michael on Mont Tombe (Mont Saint-Michel), October 16.

4. The Apparition of St. Michael on Mont Gargano, May 8.

5. Feast of the Archangel Gabriel, March 18.

6. Feast of the Archangel Raphael, October 24.

7. Feast of St. Joseph, patron of a happy death, March 19.

VI - Prayers Recommended to the Members of the Archconfraternity.

1. The daily recital of the following Invocation : — Sancte Michael, Archangele, defende nos in praelio, ut non pereamus in tremendo judicio.

"St. Michael, defend us in the day of battle, that we may not be lost at the dreadful judgement."

One hundred days' Indulgence once daily. A Plenary Indulgence once a month.

"Who is like unto God?" — Etienne, Bishop of Lausanne. Forty days' Indulgence.

2. Prayer to our Angel Guardian : — Angele Dei, qui custos es mei, me tibi commissum pietate superna, illumina, custodi, rege et guberna. Amen,

"O Angel of God, whom God hath appointed to be my guardian, enlighten and

protect me, direct and govern me. Amen."

One hundred days' Indulgence every time, and a Plenary Indulgence once a month, if said daily.

3. The *De profundis* for the dead. One hundred days' Indulgence.

4. The following invocations : — *St. Michael, Archangel, pray for us. Holy Angels, pray for us.* These two invocations alone are binding on members of the Archconfraternity.

ജ❖ഓ

APPENDIX

Other Associations, Sacramentals and Prayers in Honour of St. Michael

‍ ❖ ‍

The Confraternity of the Scapular of St. Michael

First formally approved by Pius IX, the original Confraternity was founded in 1878 in the Church of St. Eustachius at Rome, while another Confraternity was founded in 1879 in the Church of Sant' Angelo in Pescheria (Sancti Angeli in foro Piscium). In 1880 Pope Leo XIII raised the association in Sancti Angeli to the rank of Archconfraternity of the Scapular of St. Michael. Indulgences were approved by the Congregation for Indulgences in 1903. Each member of the confraternity was invested with the scapular of St. Michael. It was also associated with the Archconfraternity of St. Michael in Mont St. Michel.

Both Archconfraternities were extinguished, however, the scapular is now connected with the Congregation of St. Michael, or Michaelite Fathers founded in 1897 by Bl. Bronisław Markiewicz (1842-1912). The faithful may still receive the graces and blessings of the scapular via the blessing and investiture prayer ceremony, which can be said by any priest or deacon.

The scapular cloth pieces are distinct in shape compared with other scapulars: they are in the shape of a shield, one is dark blue, the other black. On the older traditional scapular, a picture of St. Michael is on both pieces of cloth, and features his name and battle cry: "*Quis ut Deus?*" Regarding the straps: one is blue, and the other is black.

There is now a new and approved form of the scapular that still consists of the black and blue details, but the picture on the black cloth features the image of St. Michael of Mt. Gargano, while the blue cloth features a picture of Our Lady of the shrine in Miejsce Piastowe –the Motherhouse of the Michaelites. This new form was approved on 1 March 2013 by the decree of the Superior General of the Congregation of St. Michael, Fr Kazimierz Radzik. It was also recognised and approved by Pope Benedict XVI, who wrote in his "Letter to Michaelites" that the motives of the receiving of the Scapular in its present form should serve as a reminder to the wearer that they are experiencing an effective assistance of the mighty Defender, discovering in oneself the majesty, goodness and love of God, and to realise that there is no greater value, or any other equally great good outside of God - the

Creator and Lord of all living things.

The cloth Scapular may also be substituted with the St. Michael Scapular Medal, which was approved on March 1, 2013 by the Superior General of the Congregation of St Michael. The faithful wearing the medal Scapular participate in all the spiritual privileges resulting from wearing the cloth Scapular. However, admission to the Scapular is done by investing the cloth Scapular by a priest or deacon. Then it may be exchanged for Scapular medal that has been blessed. The medal is in the form of a shield like the cloth one: one side shows the statue of St. Michael the Archangel from the Italian shrine on Mount Gargano and the inscription: "St. Michael defend us in battle.' The other side shows the coat of arms of the Congregation of St. Michael the Archangel with the inscription, 'Who is like God' and the motto 'Moderation and Work'.

The Purpose of the Scapular:

It is an outward sign of entrusting oneself to St. Michael Archangel and of belonging to the Michaelite family. The purpose of wearing it is a renewal of reverence towards the great Archangel. Those who receive the scapular share in the spiritual goods of the Congregation of St. Michael the Archangel.

The Symbolism of the Scapular

The part hanging on the back of the wearer represents the attitude of submission to the will of God in enduring hardships, difficulties and one's cross. The front part of the Scapular hanging on the chest is a reminder that the human heart should beat with love for God and neighbour, that the wearer must break away from worldly attachments and through the intercession of St. Michael strive for eternal good. Wearing the Scapular should remind one of their Christian responsibilities as a condition of certainty that St. Michael the Archangel will intercede for us. The Scapular expresses faith in the Christian encounter with God in eternal life through the intercession and protection of St. Michael the Archangel.

The Role of the Scapular

The Scapular is a sign one has chosen St. Michael as a special defender against temptation and sin. It is a uniform of the angelic army. Just as a soldier, a policeman and a priest can be distinguished by their dress, so too those belonging to the Confraternity of the Scapular can be recognized by this sign. The Scapular is its garment, and as with the role of a garment which is to protect the body the Scapular performs the same role in the spiritual life: it aids in defending the wearer from anything that might be an obstacle to the road to salvation, i.e. from sin, Satan and hell. Wearing the Scapular is a source of grace to help one bear the sacrifices and austerities that are required in the struggle against sin and in imitating Christ

The Purpose of Having the Scapular

The Scapular is a sign of the devotion to St. Michael in order to receive through his intercession: a) the freedom, the protection and development of the holy Church; b) the grace of a good confession for oneself and others; the strength in the fight against addiction and vices; defence against heresies, errors and false teachings; cessation of profanity, blasphemy and of offences; and the conversion of all sinners; c) the spirit of gentleness and humility of heart and increase of faith, hope and love; d) affirmation of the Kingdom of God in the world through the powerful intercession of Our Lady Queen of Angels and of the holy angels; e) the deliverance of souls from purgatory by the prayers and obtaining of indulgences; f) the grace of a good and holy death.

The Benefits of Receiving the Scapular

Those wearing the scapular and belonging to the Confraternity of the Scapular of Saint Michael the Archangel participate in the spiritual benefits of the Congregation of St. Michael the Archangel. The reception of the Scapular enables us to be incorporated into the Michaelite family. This is an additional grace for practising this devotion. The wearers have a share in all the spiritual benefits of the Congregation, that is, indulgences, the merits of the saints and blesseds, Holy Masses, prayers, mortifications, fasting, etc.

THE FIVE CONDITIONS for RECEIVING THE SCAPULAR and ITS BENEFITS

1. The scapular must be accepted from the hands of an authorized priest or deacon;
2. The member of the Confraternity must carry it or keep it in a dedicated space;
3. They must recite daily the simple exorcism of Pope Leo XIII. (i.e. the short daily prayer to St. Michael: "St. Michael the Archangel, defend us in battle. Be thou our safeguard against the wickedness and the snares of the devil. May God restrain him we humbly pray, and do thou, O Prince of the Heavenly Hosts, by the power

of God, cast down into Hell Satan and all his wicked spirits that wander through the world for the ruin of souls. Amen."

4. Make an act of consecration to St Michael on one Tuesday of the month during communal devotion or individually.

5. Give honour to your Choir of Angels in the month dedicated to them.

The Scapular can be received on any chosen day. However, it gains a particular importance if the reception is done on one of the feast days dedicated to St. Michael and the Holy Angels. Then the sign of the Scapular becomes even more meaningful.

The Holy Days and Celebrations that Members Must Celebrate

Those who received the Scapular, cultivating spiritual connection with the Congregation of St. Michael, in a special way are to celebrate the following feast days and celebrations:

a) Holy Archangels: Michael, Gabriel and Raphael (September 29);

b) The Holy Guardian Angels (October 2);

c) Bl. Bronisław Markiewicz, Founder of the Congregation (30 January);

d) Revelation of St. Michael the Archangel on Mount Gargano (8 May);

e) Attend the prayer meetings in the month dedicated to your Choir of Angels

How to Prepare to Receive the Scapular

Preparation should be done by attending the sacrament of confession, it is encouraged that the person be in a state of grace during the time of reception of the Scapular. This will allow the grace of God to touch even more the one who is entrusted to the care of St. Michael the Archangel. Children can receive the Scapular, however it is recommended that they are at such an age, that they can understand the basic truths of faith, preferably after their First Holy Communion.

Is it Necessary to Go Through the Rite of Investiture?

The type of the Scapular (cloth or medal) is a personal choice of the individual person. However, the participation in the graces associated with it requires the reception according to an approved Rite. Of course, anyone can put on the Scapular medal around their neck and certainly St Michael will accompany them in life. However, participation in the graces associated with this Scapular requires a formal form of reception of this sign.

The Rite of the investiture of the Scapular originates from the Shrine of St. Michael the Archangel on Mount Gargano, where it is celebrated as a form of *sacramentalia*. Reception of the Scapular can take place only once. The Scapular must be blessed in accordance with the investiture rite. The Scapular can be blessed by any priest or deacon, and they have the right to invest the faithful into the Scapular using the Rite approved by the Superior General of the Congregation of St Michael the Archangel. Investiture cannot be performed by a lay person. A layperson may give a scapular or scapular medal, but to be fully invested in the benefits of the confraternity, the person must be invested into the Confraternity by a priest or deacon.

Is Enrolment in the Book of Confraternity of the Scapular Necessary?

No, entry in the Book of the Scapular Confraternity is not a necessary condition for acceptance of the scapular and if someone does not want, does not need to make such an entry. Still, everyone receiving the Scapular is encouraged to enrol in the book and provide the basic information: name, age, place of residence. The Michaelite Fathers have a sites online where you may find information on how to enrol via the post, or, may you enrol online here (current web address existing at the time of the is publication):

https://stmichael.com/the-confraternity

Wearing and Displaying the Scapular

It is ideal that the Scapular is worn around the neck. The abundance of graces obtained through the intercession of St- Michael requires the member to wear the scapular in a dignified manner. But it can also be hidden discreetly under the clothes or in a wallet. If it is kept at home it should be placed in a reverent manner in a dedicated place of honour.

What if I Discontinue Wearing it?

To discontinue wearing the Scapular is not a sin, but the person who ceases to carry it ceases to benefit from the promised graces. If someone for a long time, even several years, does not wear the scapular and then decides to wear it again, a second investiture is not needed. They can simply start wearing it again. However: if the scapular was discarded in sinful manner with contempt, and then the person repents and converts later, that person needs to be reinvested again by a priest or deacon after having received confession and is once again in a state of grace.

What About Replacement Scapulars?

The first scapular received during the investiture must be of cloth. Then it may be replaced with the Scapular medal, if you choose to wear the medal. When the cloth Scapular is worn out or destroyed the replacement can be purchased and used straight away similar to the Brown Scapular as the blessing and investiture are attached for the whole life to the person who received it. Since they are a sacramental, worn out cloth scapulars should be burned out of respect and not thrown out into the garbage.

ജ❖ര

THE RITE of BLESSING and ENROLLEMENT in THE SCAPULAR

The full ritual, translated into English as presented in the Weller English translation of the *Rituale Romanum*, for the blessing and enrolment in the Scapular of the Archangel. The priest is to be wearing a white stole.

- V. Our help is in the name of the Lord.
- R. Who made heaven and earth.
- V. The Lord be with thee.
- R. And with thy spirit.
- Let us pray.

O Almighty, everlasting God, Who dost graciously defend thy Church from the wiles of the devil through St. Michael the Archangel, we suppliantly implore thee to bless ✠ and sanctify ✠ this token introduced for arousing and fostering devotion among thy faithful toward this great protector. And do thou grant all who wear it may be strengthened by the same holy archangel, so as to vanquish the enemies of body and soul, both in this life and at the hour of death. Through Christ our Lord.

R. Amen

The priest then sprinkles the scapular with holy water, and then bestows it, saying:

Receive brother (sister), the scapular of St. Michael the Archangel, so that by his constant intercession thou mayest be disposed to lead a holy life.

R. Amen.

Let us pray. We appeal to thy goodness, O Lord that thou wouldst hear our prayers and graciously bless ✠ this servant (handmaid) of thine, who has been placed under the special patronage of St. Michael the Archangel. Through his intercession may he (she) avoid and guard against whatever is displeasing to thee, and thus merit in serving thee to accomplish his (her) own sanctification and that of others. Through Christ our Lord. Amen

The Devotional Knights
of St. Michael the Archangel

ᔧ❖ᔤ

Not to be confused with the royal order of Portugal, this is a devotional association overseen by the Congregation of St Michael the Archangel, or Michaelites, the same order that is connected with St. Michael's Scapular Confraternity.

The official name of this apostolic movement is the Devotional Knights of Saint Michael the Archangel. The Patron Saint of the Knighthood is Saint Michael the Archangel.

Aim of the Knights

Knights are confirmed Catholics who are open to the Holy Spirit and give themselves to Christ, unite with Him, and aid the Church by helping to protect it from the attacks of the demons.

The main task of the knights is to proclaim the victory of Jesus Christ over Satan. The knights are sent on a mission to expiate the sins of human kind and to obtain the conversion of sinners. They aim to achieve this by reciting the prayer of St Michael the Archangel to defend us in the day of battle. This simple prayer of exorcism is said every day to keep away evil spirits from oneself, the Church and the whole world, particularly from those who are tempted and possessed by Satan. It is referred to in these set of the Statutes / Rules as the prayer of simple exorcism.

Knights' Participation in Spiritual Goods

All knights belong to the spiritual family of Michaelites and participate in their spiritual benefits such as:

- Masses celebrated by Michaelite Fathers on the first Tuesday of the month;

- Daily prayers of the members of the Congregation of St Michael the Archangel;

- Daily prayers to the Queen of Heaven.

Knights gain many merits for eternal life by uniting more closely with Christ, and through Him, with God the Father in the Holy Spirit, working and doing everything for the sake of His Divine love, opening to the Holy Spirit, being inspired by St Michael the Archangel and the guardian angels, accepting their help and driving away evil spirits from people by saying the prayer of simple exorcism, (i.e. the prayer of St. Michael).

- Prayers will be said for deceased knights. The General Animator celebrates Gregorian Masses each November for deceased knights. The National Animator celebrates Mass for a deceased knight just after he receives information about his or her death.

Responsibilities
of a Knight of St Michael

- The main duty of knights is the continuous effort to be in a state of grace and in friendship with God so that they can exclaim about Satan: "He has no power over me" (John 14: 30).
- All knights must respect the Holy Father, the bishops and priests and all the teachings of the Church. They should defend them if required. An attitude of humility and obedience towards God and the Church should be an obvious feature of every knight.
- All knights should pray for the growth of the Michaelite family.

The Weapons / Requirements of the Knights

- Daily Bible reading
- Daily exorcism prayer to St Michael (i.e. the prayer to St. Michael - "St. Michael the archangel, defend us in battle, be thou our safeguard..." (etc.)
- Daily angelic chaplet to St Michael
- Fast each Friday on bread and water (or a good deed if a fast is impossible)
- Monthly Reconciliation
- Monthly Eucharist Adoration
- Nine day Novena to St Michael before the feast day on 29th September.

May God help me to fulfil this devotion. St. Michael the Archangel pray for me. Amen.

Is there an Official Enrolment into the Knighthood?

No. This is a devotion and therefore there is no need for an official enrolment. However if the General Animator of the Knighthood is on a mission in a particular country and a group wishes to make their promise publicly before God then an official enrolment can take place after the Holy Mass with written prior notice given, this has happened in Ireland, the UK and the USA. Check with the website of the Michaelites to find out if the General Animator is visiting your country and how such an enrolment could be scheduled:

http://stmichaelthearchangel.info/knighthood.shtml

TO BECOME A KNIGHT

The person wishing to become a knight must first consider if they are willing or able to fulfil the all the conditions above before making the 'Promise' to be a knight.

Perhaps the bread and water fast on Fridays is too much, especially if you have an illness and you can opt to perform a good deed instead, etc., or, you might have time and work restrictions attempting to fulfil the prayer and Bible reading requirements, or, perhaps you can only go to Confession twice a month, etc. People usually give themselves a two to three month period to find out if they can fulfil all the requirements. This is the 'trial' period.

If the person is then willing to fulfil this to become a knight, they can then make their promise.

THE PROMISE:

"I, (your name) a repentant sinner, renounce Satan and resolve to follow Jesus Christ. I express my faith in the Holy Trinity and the Holy Church. After my trial period, today in the presence of God, St Michael and the Holy Angels, I promise to be a Knight of St Michael to the end of my life and to take part in the spiritual battle for the salvation of souls. I entrust myself to St Michael as my Patron and Protector in this devotion."

The Devotional of the Knights of St Michael the Archangel was approved on 15th August 2013.
Fr Kazimierz Tomaszewski CSMA, Superior General approved this version two of the original Knighthood, which was approved on 8th July 2003.

(Information about the Knights from the Michaelite Website.)

ഔ❖ଓ

The SIMPLE EXORCISM of Pope Leo XIII

A Prayer Against Satan for Priests or Laity

Prayer Against Satan
and the Rebellious Angels.

Published by Order of His Holiness Pope Leo XIII, (adjusted to conform with "Inde Ab Aliquot Annis" of 29 September 1985.)

The following is a simple exorcism prayer that can be said by priests or laity. The term "exorcism" does not always denote a solemn exorcism involving a person possessed by the devil. In general, the term denotes prayers to "curb the power of the devil and prevent him from doing harm." As Saint Peter had written in Holy Scripture, "your adversary the devil, as a roaring lion, goeth about seeking whom he may devour." (1 Saint Peter 5:8)

The Holy Father exhorts priests to say this prayer as often as possible, as a simple exorcism to curb the power of the devil and prevent him from doing harm. The faithful also may say it in their own name, for the same purpose, as any approved prayer, (i.e. for private use). Its use is recommended whenever action of the devil is suspected, causing malice in men, violent temptations and even storms and various calamities. It *could* be used as a solemn exorcism (an official and public ceremony, in Latin), to expel the devil. *It would then be said by a priest, in the name of the Church and only with a Bishop's permission*

Beginning Prayer to Saint Michael the Archangel.

In the Name of the Father, and of the Son, and of the Holy Ghost. Amen.

Most glorious Prince of the Heavenly Armies, Saint Michael the Archangel, defend us in "our battle against principalities and powers, against the rulers of this world of darkness, against the spirits of wickedness in the high places" (Ephes, 6:12). Come to the assistance of men whom God has created to His likeness and whom He has redeemed at a great price from the tyranny of the devil. Holy Church venerates thee as her guardian and protector; to thee, the Lord has entrusted the souls of the redeemed to be led into heaven. Pray therefore the God of Peace to crush Satan beneath our feet, that he may no longer retain men captive and do injury to the Church. Offer our prayers to the Most High, that without delay they may draw His mercy down upon us; take hold of "the dragon, the old serpent, which is the devil and Satan", bind him and cast him into the bottomless pit ... "that he may no longer seduce the nations" (Apoc 20:2-3).

Exorcism

In the Name of Jesus Christ, our God and Lord, strengthened by the intercession of the Immaculate Virgin Mary, Mother of God, of Blessed Michael the Archangel, of the Blessed Apostles Peter and Paul and all the Saints, (*This part said by priests only*: 'and powerful in the holy authority of our ministry') we confidently undertake to repulse the attacks and deceits of the devil.

(Psalm 67: 2-3) God arises; His enemies are scattered and those who hate Him flee before Him. As smoke is driven away, so are they driven; as wax melts before the fire, so the wicked perish at the presence of God.

V. Behold the Cross of the Lord, flee bands of enemies.
R. He has conquered, the Lion of the tribe of Judah, the offspring of David.
V. May Thy mercy, Lord, descend upon us.
R. As great as our hope in Thee.

(*The crosses below ✠ indicate a blessing is to be given if a priest recites the Exorcism; if a lay person recites it, the Sign of the Cross is to be made silently by that person.*)

We drive you from us, whoever you may be, unclean spirits, all satanic powers, all infernal invaders, all wicked legions, assemblies and sects. In the name and by the power of Our Lord Jesus Christ, ✠ may you be snatched away and driven from the Church of God and from the souls made in the image and likeness of God and redeemed by the Precious Blood of the Divine Lamb. ✠ Most cunning serpent, you shall no more dare to deceive the human race, persecute the Church, torment God's elect and sift them as wheat. ✠ The Most High God commands you. ✠ He with whom, in your great insolence, you still claim to be equal. "He who wants all men to be saved and to come to the knowledge of the truth" (1 Tim., II), God the Father commands you. ✠ God the Son commands you. ✠ God the Holy Spirit commands you. ✠ Christ, God's Word made Flesh commands you; ✠ He who to save our race outdone through your envy "humbled Himself, becoming obedient even unto death" (Phil., II, 8); He who has built His Church on a firm rock and declared that "the gates of hell shall not prevail against Her, because He will dwell with Her all days even to the end of the world" (St. Mark XXVIII, 20) The Sacred Sign of the Cross commands you, ✠ as does also the power of the mysteries of the Christian faith. ✠ The glorious Mother of God, the Virgin Mary, commands you; ✠ She who by her humility and from the first moment of her Immaculate Conception crushed your proud head. The faith of the Holy Apostles Peter and Paul and of the other Apostles commands you. ✠ The blood of the Martyrs and the pious intercession of all the Saints command you. ✠

Thus, cursed dragon, and you diabolical legions, we adjure you by the living God, ✠ by the true God, ✠ by the holy God, ✠ by the God "who so loved the world that He gave up His only Son, that every soul believing in Him might not perish but have life everlasting" (St. John, III); stop deceiving human creatures and pouring out to them the poison of eternal damnation; stop harming (*name*) and the Church and hindering her liberty. Begone, Satan, inventor and master of all deceit, enemy of man's salvation. Give place to Christ in whom you have found none of your works; give place to the One, Holy and Apostolic Church acquired by Christ at the price of His Blood. Stoop beneath the all-powerful Hand of God; tremble and flee when we invoke the Holy and terrible Name of Jesus, the Name which causes hell to tremble, this Name to which the Virtues, Powers and Dominations of heaven are humbly submissive, this Name the Cherubim and Seraphim praise unceasingly repeating: Holy, Holy, Holy is the Lamb, the God of Armies.

V. O Lord, hear my prayer.

R. And let my cry come unto Thee.

V. May the Lord be with thee. [or: May the Lord be with us.]

R. And with your spirit. [or: And with our spirits.]

Let us pray.

God of heaven, God of earth, God of Angels, God of Archangels, God of Patriarchs, God of Prophets, God of Apostles, God of Martyrs, God of Confessors, God of Virgins, God who has power to give life after death and rest after work: because there is no other God than Thee and there can be no other, for Thou art the Creator of all things, visible and invisible, of Whose reign there shall be no end, we humbly prostrate ourselves before Thy glorious Majesty and we beseech Thee to deliver us by Thy power from all the tyranny of the infernal spirits, from their snares, their lies and their furious wickedness. Deign, O Lord, to grant us Thy powerful protection and to keep us safe and sound. We beseech Thee through Jesus Christ Our Lord. Amen.

V. From the snares of the devil,

R. Deliver us, O Lord.

V. That Thy Church may serve Thee in peace and liberty:

R. We beseech Thee to hear us.

V. That Thou may crush down all enemies of Thy Church:

R. We beseech Thee to hear us.

(*Holy water is sprinkled in the place where we may be.*)

END OF THE EXORCISM PRAYER

Saint Michael the Archangel, defend us in the battle; be our protection against the malice and snares of the devil. May God restrain him, we humbly pray, and do thou, O Prince of the heavenly host, by the divine power, cast into hell Satan and all the other evil spirits who roam through the world seeking the ruin of souls. Amen.

Most Sacred Heart of Jesus, have mercy on us.

ಸಿ ❖ ೂ

Prayer for the Church and For Souls

(Roman Raccolta, July 23, 1898,
supplement approved July 31, 1902.)

O Glorious Prince of the heavenly host, St. Michael the Archangel, defend us in the battle and in the terrible warfare that we are waging against the principalities and powers, against the rulers of this world of darkness, against the evil spirits. Come to the aid of man, whom Almighty God created immortal, made in His own image and likeness, and redeemed at a great price from the tyranny of Satan.

Fight this day the battle of the Lord, together with the holy angels, as already thou hast fought the leader of the proud angels, Lucifer, and his apostate host, who were powerless to resist thee, nor was there place for them any longer in Heaven. That cruel, ancient serpent, who is called the devil or Satan who seduces the whole world, was cast into the abyss with his angels. Behold, this primeval enemy and slayer of men has taken courage. Transformed into an angel of light, he wanders about with all the multitude of wicked spirits, invading the earth in order to blot out the name of God and of His Christ, to seize upon, slay and cast into eternal perdition souls destined for the crown of eternal glory. This wicked dragon pours

out, as a most impure flood, the venom of his malice on men of depraved mind and corrupt heart, the spirit of lying, of impiety, of blasphemy, and the pestilent breath of impurity, and of every vice and iniquity.

These most crafty enemies have filled and inebriated with gall and bitterness the Church, the spouse of the immaculate Lamb, and have laid impious hands on her most sacred possessions. In the Holy Place itself, where the See of Holy Peter and the Chair of Truth has been set up as the light of the world, they have raised the throne of their abominable impiety, with the iniquitous design that when the Pastor has been struck, the sheep may be scattered.

Arise then, O invincible Prince, bring help against the attacks of the lost spirits to the people of God, and give them the victory. They venerate thee as their protector and patron; in thee holy Church glories as her defence against the malicious power of hell; to thee has God entrusted the souls of men to be established in heavenly beatitude. Oh, pray to the God of peace that He may put Satan under our feet, so far conquered that he may no longer be able to hold men in captivity and harm the Church. Offer our prayers in the sight of the Most High, so that they may quickly find mercy in the sight of the Lord; and vanquishing the dragon, the ancient serpent, who is the devil and Satan, do thou again make him captive in the abyss, that he may no longer seduce the nations. Amen.

V. Behold the Cross of the Lord; be scattered ye hostile powers.

R. The Lion of the tribe of Judah has conquered, the root of David.

V. Let Thy mercies be upon us, O Lord.

R. As we have hoped in Thee.

V. O Lord, hear my prayer.

R. And let my cry come unto Thee.

Let us pray.

O God, the Father of our Lord Jesus Christ, we call upon Thy holy Name, and as supplicants, we implore Thy clemency, that by the intercession of Mary, ever Virgin Immaculate and our Mother, and of the glorious St. Michael the Archangel, Thou wouldst deign to help us against Satan and all the other unclean spirits who wander about the world for the injury of the human race and the ruin of souls. Amen.

৪০ ❖ ৫৪

A Prayer for Help
Against Spiritual Enemies

Glorious Saint Michael, Prince of the heavenly hosts, who stands always ready to give assistance to the people of God; who fought with the dragon, the old serpent, and cast him out of heaven, and now valiantly defends the Church of God that the gates of hell may never prevail against her, I earnestly entreat you to assist me also, in the painful and dangerous conflict which I sustain against the same formidable foe.

Be with me, O mighty Prince! that I may courageously fight and vanquish that proud spirit, whom you, by the Divine Power, gloriously overthrew, and whom our powerful King, Jesus Christ, has, in our nature, completely overcome; so having triumphed over the enemy of my salvation, I may with you and the holy angels, praise the clemency of God who, having refused mercy to the rebellious angels after their fall, has granted repentance and forgiveness to fallen man. Amen.

৯০ ❖ ୧୪

శ్రీ ❖ ಆ

Prayer for Protection
of the Church and Her Members

O glorious St. Michael, guardian and defender of the Church of Jesus Christ, come to the assistance of this Church, against which the powers of hell are unchained, guard with especial care her august Head, and obtain that for him and for us the hour of triumph may speedily arrive. O glorious Archangel St. Michael, watch over us during life, defend us against the assaults of the demon, assist us especially at the hour of death; obtain for us a favourable judgement, and the happiness of beholding God face to face for endless ages.   Amen.

శ్రీ ❖ ಆ

Indulgenced Invocations

"Saint Michael the archangel, defend us in the battle, that we may not perish in the fearful judgement." - *(From the Roman Missal. 300 days indulgence, a plenary indulgence under the usual conditions for the devout recitation of this invocation every day for a month.)*

"Saint Michael, first champion of the Kingship of Christ, pray for us." - *(300 days indulgence.)*

Also, the faithful who recite devoutly some prayers in honour of St. Michael the Archangel at any season of the year, with the intention of continuing the said prayers for nine successive days, may gain an indulgence of 5 years once each day.

FINIS

Illustration Credits

Cover, Page 28 - *"St. Michael"* by Carl Rahl (1834) - Stiftskirche Reichersberg, Oberösterreich Hochaltar von 1713 (unter Verwendung älterer Figuren). Photo by Andreas Praefcke (2010), released by the photographer into the Public Domain, Wikimedia Commons.

Page 32 - *"Abraham and the Three Angels"* (c. 1750) by Francesco Fontebasso. Los Angeles County Museum of Art.

Page 34 - *"Abraham's Sacrifice"* (1655) by Rembrandt van Rijn. Art Institute of Chicago.

Page 39 - *"Jacob Wrestling with the Angel"* (c. 1601–68) attributed to Giulio Benso. Metropolitan Museum of Art, New York.

Page 40 - *"Moses and the Burning Bush"* by Gerard Hoet (1648–1733). Metropolitan Museum of Art, New York.

Page 46 - *"St Michael"* (c. 1610-1649) by Pietro Testa. SMK – Statens Museum for Kunst, Denmark.

Page 50 - *"Joshua and the Angel"* (c. 1851- 1860). Woodcut by Julius Schnorr von Carolsfeld. Wikimedia Commons - Copyright- PD-US- Expired / Public Domain.

Page 55 - *"The Angel Appearing to Gideon"* (1561), Plate 1 in 'The Story of Gideon' series. Engraving after Maerten van Heemskerck (1498-1574). Los Angeles County Museum of Art.

Page 61 - *"L'Ange de saint Matthieu (Bartsch 73)"*, by Martin Schongauer, Martin (1485 et 1491), engraved by Colmar c1450- 1491). Petit Palais, musée des Beaux-arts de la Ville de Paris. Paris Mussées Collections - CC 0 – 1.0.

Page 67 - *"Destruction of the Army of Sennacherib"* by Gustave Doré. Public Domain Illustration provided by www.creationism.org/images

Page 70 - "*Saint Michael and the Rebel Angels*" (c. 1682) by Gregorio De Ferrari. National Gallery of Art.

Page 72 - "*The Holy Trinity with Saint Michael Conquering the Dragon*" (1666) by Pietro da Cortona. Art Institute of Chicago.

Page 75 - "*Heliodorus cast from the Temple*" by Gustave Doré. Public Domain Illustration provided by www.creationism.org/images

Page 78 - "Agony in the Garden" (c. 1660–1719?) by Benoit Thiboust after Carlo Maratti. Metropolitan Museum of Art.

Page 81 - "*The Resurrection*" by Gustave Doré
Public Domain Illustration provided by
www.creationism.org/images

Page 85 - "*Angel appearing to Peter in Prison*" (c. 1680–1743) Robert van Audenaerde after Carlo Maratti. Metropolitan Museum of Art.

Page 86 - "St. Michael with Sword" (c. 1613 – 1661). Public Domain, Rijksmuseum API Collectie, Amsterdam.

Page 89 - "*St. Michael and the Angels Taking the Body of Moses*", Illustration in "The Bible and its story" (1908). Public Domain, Wikimedia Commons / Internet Archive.

Page 90 - '*Et vidi alium angelum fortem... ('And I saw a strong angel') The Angel of the Apocalypse Appearing to Saint John)*" (1809/1810) by Luigi Sabatelli. National Gallery of Art.

Page 96 - "*The Woman clothed with Sun - St. Michael casting Down the Dragon*" by Gustave Doré. Public Domain Illustration provided by www.creationism.org/images

Page 103 - "*St. Michael the Archangel*" (c. 1660s) by Claudio Coello. Frick Digital Collections – Public Domain.

Page 111 - "The Resurrection" (1586) from "The Passion of the Christ" by Hendrick Goltzius. Metropolitan Museum of Art, New York.

Page 114 - "*Legend of Mt. Gargano*", Part 1 from the "*Scenes from the Legend of St. Michael*" by the Master of Palanquinos, active approximately 1450-1475. Frick Digital Collections - Public Domain.

Page 119 - "*Mont Saint Michel*" - Originalzeichnung von R. Püttner. From page 673 of the journal "*Die Gartenlaube*" (1887). Wikimedia Commons – Public Domain.

Page 124 - French lead pilgrim badge of St. Michael slaying the dragon, date c. 14th to 16th century. Metropolitan Museum of Art, Cloisters Collection (1977). Photograph released into the Public Domain.

Page 127 - Front and Back views of a double-sided Gold Badge of the French Royal Order of St. Michael,
(17th century).   Metropolitan Museum of Art. Photographs released into the Public Domain.

Page 138 - "*Saints Michael and Francis*" (c. 1505–9) by Juan de Flandes. Metropolitan Museum of Art, New York.

Page 144 - "*Saint Michael*" (Coming to the Aid of a Dying Christian), by Josef Christ (c. 1732-1788). Metropolitan Museum of Art.

Page 152 - "*Michael and the Dragon*", woodcut in "*Die Bibel in Bildern*" by Julius Schnorr von Carolsfeld, (c. 1860). Wikimedia Commons, Public Domain Image.

Page 156 - "*St. Michael*" by Guido Reni (1575-1642). Public Domain Photograph from the Frick Digital Collections.

Page 161 - "*St. Michael Conquering Satan*" (c. 17th century). Anonymous painting from the Bolognese Italian School. Frick Digital Collections.

Page 163 - "*The Nine Choirs of Celestial Spirits*" (1679) by Louis Licherie- Frick Digital Collections.

Page 177 – "St. Michael Presenting His Arms to the Virgin

Mary" by Louis Le Nain (1593-1648). Frick Digital Collections.

Page 178 - "*St. Michael the Archangel*" (c. 1640s) by Ignacio de Ries. Metropolitan Museum of Art.

Page 183 - "*The Archangel Michael*" (c. 1624-1626) Cavaliere d'Arpino. Minneapolis Institute of Art.

Page 190 - "*St. Michael the Archangel and St. Bernard with a Cistercian Monk*" (c. 1497) by Bernardo Zenale. Frick Digital Collections.

Page 203 - "*Old Italian Masters: St. Michael, 1888-1892*", wood engraving by Timothy Cole. Cleveland Museum of Art.

Page 210 - "*Saint Michael*" (c. 1450-1467) by Master Es. Cleveland Museum of Art.

Page 219 - "*Saint Michael*" by Agostino Veneziano (Agostino dei Musi) after Raphael, (c. 1514-1516). Metropolitan Museum of Art, New York.

Page 222 - "*St. Michael*" by Palomino de Castro and Antonio Velasco, (1655-1726). Frick Digital Collections.

Page 225 - "*St Michael*", (c. 1600-1640). Anonymous etching a painting by Guido Reni. Metropolitan Museum of Art.

www.ingramcontent.com/pod-product-compliance
Lightning Source LLC
Chambersburg PA
CBHW021051090426
42738CB00006B/286